THE JESUS GENERATION

BILLY GRAHAM

THE JESUS GENERATION

HODDER AND STOUGHTON
LONDON SYDNEY AUCKLAND TORONTO

Grateful acknowledgment is made to the following for permission to use copyrighted material: Quotations from TIME are reprinted by permission from TIME, The Weekly Newsmagazine, © Time, Inc. Quotations from LOOK are reprinted by permission from LOOK, © Cowles Communications, Inc.

To my three wonderful daughters
Virginia, Anne, and Bunny
and
to three exceptional sons-in-law
Stephan, Danny, and Ted

CONTENTS

Preface

PREFACE

There are all kinds of revolutions going on throughout the world at this moment — political, social, moral, scientific, violent — you name it!

This book is about two revolutions — the "youth revolution" and the "Jesus revolution."

Revolution means "change," and our world is changing so fast that few of us can keep up with it. Possibly the most outstanding revolution now taking place in America is what *Time* magazine calls "The Jesus Revolution." And it is not confined to America. There are signs that it is beginning in many other countries as well. But tens of thousands of American youth are caught up in it. They are being "turned on" to Jesus. People everywhere ask me such questions as: Is it genuine? What brought it about? Will it last? Are the youth really getting the old-time religion? Is it deep enough? What about the rock opera "Jesus Christ Superstar"?

I am bombarded with such questions through the mail, in private conversations, and at press conferences. I've been asked about it on Capitol Hill and at the White House. I've discussed it with the editors of the *New York Times*, the *Chicago Tribune*, and many others. Everyone is interested in this phenomenon.

The spiritual awakening among youth has been going on for several years, but only recently has it been discovered and glamorized by the press. Many organizations working with young people have detected this new spiritual interest during the last ten years. In the early sixties we suddenly began to realize that our crusades were comprised largely of youth, which was a drastic change from the fifties.

Thus, I feel compelled to answer some of the questions put to me by the press, young people, youth counselors, parents, teachers, and even psychologists. In THE JESUS GENERATION I have written about the problems and hang-ups that are bugging the young. At times I have tried to analyze the young for their parents so that parents and teachers can have a better understanding of this emerging generation.

Therefore, this book is not only *to* the young, *about* the young, and *for* the young, but it is also for the older generation to help them in bridging the generation gap.

Almost every young person I know is caught up in some sort of a revolution. It may be hidden and deeply personal or it may be openly active and highly public!

Most young people are searching for purpose, meaning, and fulfillment in their lives. I have written this book to answer those questions which millions of young people, consciously or unconsciously, are asking.

I wrote the original manuscript for this book while on a small island in the Caribbean. I sent it to my long-time friend, Curtis Mitchell, who had already done some research for me. He revamped it and made valuable suggestions, after which I did some rewriting. I then sent the material to my colleague Dr. John Wesley White. He made many changes and suggestions, including a rearrangement of chapters.

Late in the summer I hid myself away with my wife, my youngest son, and my lifelong friends, T. W. and Grady Wilson, to again rework the manuscript. My faithful secretary, Martha Warkentin, patiently typed and retyped. Eventually we sent it to the Zondervan Publishing House. The Zondervans have been my personal friends and supporters since the beginning of my ministry.

This book, written over a period of eight months, had to be constantly updated and revised because of the changing situation among the youth. While I was working on the book, *Time, Look, Life,* and many other magazines and newspapers began carrying feature stories on what I already knew was taking place — and on what I was writing about.

I have become convinced that the "Jesus revolution" is making a profound impact on the youth of America and shows all signs of spreading to other countries. One thing is certain: Jesus Christ can no longer be ignored! Our generation cannot escape Him. We cannot dismiss Him as a myth or a figment of the imagination.

It is my prayer that in this book thousands of young people will find some answers — that parents, teachers, psychologists, sociologists, and all those who deal with young people, will find some help. But most of all, it is my prayer that through reading this book many will come to "experience" Jesus.

BILLY GRAHAM

Minneapolis, Minnesota
September 1, 1971

INTRODUCTION
THE
JESUS
REVOLUTION

The year 1971 was only a few hours old. As Grand Marshal of the Tournament of Roses Parade in Pasadena, California, I was involved in one of the most brilliant extravaganzas that America puts on every year. As my wife and I rode to the Rose Bowl Football Classic, I scanned the faces of the one and a half million people who had gathered along the parade route.

On this festive occasion one could not help but wish that the doom encroaching upon our country would vanish. For a moment I almost felt it would. But in all honesty, despite the joyous smiles, the fanfare, the flag-waving, and the singing of "America the Beautiful," I knew in my heart that decadence had settled in — that America and the world were in deep trouble.

As *Look* writer Jack Shepard put it that first week of January, 1971: "The frontiers died. America, speeding on the wit of her people, stopped inside. Like an unwatched bull whose horns grow into his skull and drive him insane, America turned on herself. We gorged and fattened. We rioted and assassinated. We shot and cursed and burned and polluted and stomped. And we lost the American vision. America today smells of despair."

I have seldom had such mixed emotions as I had that day in Pasadena. As I savored the grandeur of this great nation, I also sensed its sickness. Having invested a generation of my life in its spiritual welfare, I was watching the horizon for a cloud of impending revival to restore its spiritual greatness.

And suddenly we were made dramatically aware that a brand-new spiritual awakening was on the way. As we passed through street after street, we saw hundreds of young people, with clenched fist and raised index finger lifted upward, shouting religious slogans. Many carried placards that read: "God is Love"; "Join the spiritual revolution now"; "Love thy neighbor"; and many more. Thousands shouted their encouragement to us. Whether they wore bell-bottoms, levis, or maxis, hundreds of these young people carried Bibles.

I had an almost irrepressible urge to get into the street and identify with them. Spontaneously I returned that upward gesture and shouted to the crowds: "One Way — the Jesus Way!"

Later that month NBC ran a national television news story on the Jesus Movement, as did CBS in April. During the first week in February *Look* magazine featured a cover article in which it was announced, "The Jesus movement is upon us. . . . It shows every sign . . . of becoming a national preoccupation." The article described how "thousands and thousands of young people, upper, middle-class kids and often formerly very spaced-out kids, have obviously found an inner, very real religion." It gave testimonies in unorthodox language: "I'm stoned on Jesus. Only it's far better than being stoned. Drugs are a 'down.' This is the most incredible 'up' in the world. I feel like I'm floating all the time, with Jesus." So impressive was the movement that two of the three in the *Look* team were themselves converted, and the third conceded, "It is unquestionably the most remarkable week of my life. They had the best sounding music I've ever heard. Everyone wanted me to accept Christ too. I haven't decided yet, but I'm thinking about it." According to the *Yale Standard,* that article elicited a larger affirmative response than *Look* had received for any story in ten years.

By May, *Life* carried a cover story on the movement that

was revolutionizing the youth scene in a high-class suburb of New York. Entitled "The Groovy Christians of Rye, New York," it described one astonished father as sighing that the movement simply "transforms its converts. . . . These kids had already bugged us with every kind of classic adolescent rebellion. We'd been through long hair, peace marches, macrobiotic diets, meditation — drugs, too, of course. Now along comes this which seems to be solving all their problems from the cosmic to the trivial."

By June, *Time* was running a twelve-page cover story entitled "The Jesus Revolution," comprehensively covering the movement throughout the country, where it estimated the "number in the hundreds of thousands nationally, conceivably many more, but any figure is a guess," and stating that the tidal wave had by no means as yet crested. "The New Rebel Cry: Jesus Is Coming!" ran the red-lettered headline over the article.

By July, NBC had devoted one entire "Today Show" to a discussion of the religious revival among American young people.

What the secular media was just finding out had already been going on for several years. Various organizations working with young people, such as Fellowship of Christian Athletes, Campus Crusade for Christ, the Inter-Varsity Christian Fellowship, Young Life, Youth for Christ, the Navigators, and many others, had already found that young people by the thousands were turning to Christ. Young evangelists began to emerge, preaching the Gospel in the contemporary language of modern youth.

There was a new underground Christian press that numbered fifty newspapers across the country — for example, the *Hollywood Free Paper,* with circulation in excess of 1,000,000 a month. These encouraging developments in America had been happening at the same time that other thousands of young people were "copping out" with sex, drugs, and violence.

A social critic recently interviewed on an NBC news program said that the violent revolutionary movement in America has become stagnated and apathetic, that it is losing its steam. The movement now gathering steam, he said, is this spiritual movement among young people. *Time* magazine says there is a morning freshness to this movement, a buoyant atmosphere of hope and love along with the usual rebel zeal. Some converts seem to enjoy translating their faith into everyday life, like those who answer the phone with "Jesus loves you" instead of "hello." But their love seems more sincere than a slogan, deeper than the fast-fading sentiments of the flower children.

While many of these young people are proclaiming that Jesus was "the first hippie," *the vast majority of them are genuine in their commitment.* Most of the characteristics of the Jesus revolution are good — but there are also some dangers!

There are pitfalls. There are fears. There are critics. Some say it is too superficial — and in some cases it is. Some say it is too emotional — and in some cases it is. Some say it is outside the established church — and in some cases it is. But even in the early church such problems were encountered. However, I have tried to study this movement, and there are several commendable features that stand out. One of the interesting things is that it is spontaneous. No one leader has emerged.

The movement, thus far, centers in Jesus. With Paul in his writing to the Corinthians, these young Christians seem to be possessed with a determination to concentrate entirely on Jesus Christ Himself and the fact of His death on the cross. Paul remonstrated with the Corinthians for splitting into sects in which some said, "I belong to Paul"; others, "I belong to Apollos"; and yet others, "I belong to Cephas (Peter)." Others gloried in their baptism. Paul wanted them to focus on Jesus.

"All the Christians agree Christ is the great common denominator of the movement. He brings everyone together," observes *Look.* "Jesus is alive and well" indicates *Time,* "and living in the radiant spiritual fervor of a growing number of young Americans who have proclaimed an extraordinary religious revolution in His Name. . . . If any one mark clearly identifies them, it is their total belief in an awesome, supernatural Jesus Christ, not just a marvelous man who lived 2,000 years ago, but a living God who is both Savior and Judge, the Ruler of their destinies." Sums up *Life*, "They feel Christ as an immediate presence."

The movement is Bible-based. Notes *Life* of these "groovy Christians": they "see the Bible as the irrefutably accurate Word of God . . . solving all their problems from the cosmic to the trivial. For them, as one father observes, it's the ultimate 'how-to' Book, like the very ambitious manual of an automobile mechanic." The article continues, "Their message: The Bible is true, miracles happen, God really did so love the world that He gave it His only begotten Son," and goes on to describe that wherever they are, "Bibles abound, whether the fur-covered King James Version or scruffy back-pocket paperbacks; they are invariably well-thumbed and often memorized." This sounds like the believers of Berea, of whom Luke recorded in the Acts, "they received the message with great eagerness, studying the Scriptures every day to see whether it was as they said."

Another characteristic of the movement is the demand for an "experience" with Jesus Christ. These young people are not just students of the Bible. They emphasize that you have to have an encounter with Jesus Christ to be a Christian. Jesus Himself said, "You must be born again." He said, "Except ye be converted, and become as little children, ye shall not enter into the kingdom of heaven" (Matthew 18:3).

Time says, "Their lives revolve around the necessity for an intense personal relationship with that Jesus and the belief that such a relationship should condition every human life." These encounters with Christ that young people are having take various forms. The same article goes on to note that "many conversions seem to be . . . slow, but finally confident turn-arounds rather than lightning-bolt illuminations. Yet some do come suddenly. Marsha Daigle, Catholic and a doctoral student at the University of Michigan, was deeply distraught at the deaths of Martin Luther King, Jr. and Robert Kennedy. One day she opened a Bible and suddenly "knew Christ was my personal Savior. It was the last thing I expected."

These young people are putting a renewed emphasis on the Holy Spirit. Ten years ago I asked Dr. Karl Barth what the new emphasis in theology would be during the next twenty years. He replied without hesitation, "The Holy Spirit." Little did I dream it would come through a youth revival in America. There is no doubt that some are going to extremes, yet on the other hand a renewed emphasis on the person and work of the Holy Spirit, based upon sound Biblical study, had to come if we were to have a genuine spiritual awakening in America.

The texts that the young people are quoting are the ones like, "Not by might, nor by power, but by my spirit, saith the Lord" (Zechariah 4:6), and "For our gospel came not unto you in word only, but also in power, and in the Holy Ghost, and in much assurance" (1 Thessalonians 1:5).

"Jesus rock" singer Larry Norman exults, "a spiritual renaissance is taking place today. The Holy Spirit is at the root of it." Before He ascended into Heaven, Jesus Christ said: "And I will pray the Father, and he shall give you another Comforter, that he may abide with you for ever; Even the Spirit of truth . . . ye know him; for he dwelleth with you, and shall be in you" (John 14:16-17). During His lifetime on earth, Christ's presence could be experienced only by a small group of men at any given time. Now Christ dwells, through the Spirit, in the hearts of all those who have received Him as Savior.

These young people are finding a cure for drugs and other vicious habits which increasingly are captivating and enslaving the youth of the world.

One of the great drug experts in America told me recently that the only certain cure for drug addiction he had found was a religious experience. Many newspaper and magazine articles are saying the same thing. One magazine reported "a thirty-second cure from heroin without withdrawal pains," pointing up the testimony of E. Nathan Johnson, Acting Director, Department of Youth Service for Metropolitan Dade County, Florida (Miami is one of the worst heroin centers in the United States). He wrote that the Jesus people have found "the only lasting answer to the problems created by (drugs)." He added his wish, "May this movement spread rapidly across the nation that many thousands of the youth of this nation may be spared the ravages of the drug scene."

The emphasis in this movement is on Christian discipleship. This spiritual revolutionary movement among American young people is calling for Christian discipleship. It is not so much the wearing or the carrying of crosses which has impressed the nation, but the actual discipleship that has become characteristic of many of these young people.

Time admires their "embracing the most persistent symbol of purity, selflessness, and brotherly love in the history of Western man. . . . They subscribe to the Ten Commandments rather than to the situation ethics of the new morality. They all insist that premarital sex and drugs are out, and many have quite strict rules."

Another characteristic is the evidence of social responsibility. The movement is entirely interracial. It embraces everyone, regardless of race. "It cuts across nearly all the social dividing lines," says one magazine. "Many Jews have also joined, claiming that they are not quitting but fulfilling their Judaism."

In Acts 2 we read that the early Christians "met constantly to hear the apostles teach, to share the common life, to break bread, and to pray. A sense of awe was everywhere, and many marvels and signs were brought about through the apostles. All whose faith had drawn them together held everything in common; they would sell their property and possessions and make a general distribution as the need of each required."

Two of the things which have driven many of the youth into hippiedom and radicalism are the soulless materialism and the deification of technology in America. These young people have solved that problem by their commitment to Jesus Christ — and their commitment to each other! *Time* magazine tells of a typical meeting on the West Coast where "the hat is passed with a new invitation: 'If you have something to spare, give; if you need, take.' Finally they rise, take one another's hands, and sing, 'They'll know we are Christians by our love.'"

Nor is this shared concern directed only to the welfare of other young Christians. It is disseminated to the social and moral "rejects" from society, and while others may talk more about the social implications of the Gospel, the new youth movement is out doing something about it!

The Jesus revolution displays an incredible zeal for evangelism.

Jesus' last words on earth were: "Go forth to every part of the world and proclaim the Good News," and we read that those original Jesus people, most of them young, "went out to make their proclamation everywhere, and the Lord worked with them and confirmed their words by the miracles that followed."

One informal-styled church in California saw 15,000 youth make commitments in two years. Another in Texas had 1,000 in two weeks, and one in Florida had 500 in one week. Even hundreds of ministers are joining the Jesus Revolution.

Time says, "They are afire with a Pentecostal passion for sharing their new vision with others. Fresh-faced, wide-eyed young girls and earnest young men badger businessmen and shoppers on Hollywood Boulevard, near the Lincoln Memorial in Washington, in Dallas, in Detroit, and in Wichita, witnessing for Christ with breathless exhortations."

These young people go everywhere preaching the Gospel — into dives, slums, ghettos, theaters, record shops, and even in the underground.

Finally, the Jesus revolution has brought a reemphasis on the Second Coming of Jesus Christ. It is refreshing to see *Time's* article entitled "The New Rebel Cry: Jesus Is Coming!" and read, "There exists a firmer conviction that Jesus' Second Coming is literally at hand."

These young people don't put much stock in the old slogans of the New Deal, the Fair Deal, the New Frontier, and the Great Society. They believe that utopia will arrive only when Jesus returns. Thus these young people are on sound Biblical ground. In more than three hundred places in the New Testament alone we are taught that Jesus is coming back. History is going somewhere. God can bring beauty from the ashes of world chaos, and a new world is going to be born. A new social order will emerge when Christ comes back to set up His Kingdom. Swords will be turned into plowshares, and the lion will lie down with the lamb.

Some people say that this movement is a fad, and there is no doubt that there are faddish elements in it. At the same time, in the middle of it, thousands of these young people truly are being converted to Jesus Christ. It is my prayer that they will get quickly into the Word of God so that they can grow in the grace and knowledge of Jesus Christ. We are taught in the Scriptures that every time there is a spiritual movement, Satan is busy sowing tares and raising up false prophets and teachers to lead the uninstructed away from true faith.

At this moment the greatest need among these converts throughout America is Bible study and the teaching of the discipline of the Christian life. There is evidence that this is taking place in many parts of the country as young people are beginning to gather for Bible study and prayer.

But I do not want to leave the impression that the ma-

jority of American young people are suddenly turning to Christ. It is still a minority, but it is growing rapidly. It may be the answer to the prayers of millions of Christians who have been praying for spiritual awakening.

The vast majority of American young people are still alienated, uncommitted, and uninvolved. There is a deep vacuum within them. They are searching for individual identity. They are searching for a challenge and a faith. Whoever captures the imagination of the youth of our generation will change the world. Youth movements of the past have been perverted and led by dictators and demagogues. Perhaps the American young people will be captured by Jesus Christ.

It is to that alienated, rebellious, uncommitted majority that most of this book is directed — those who are enduring "the changing scene" and "bad vibrations."

1
THE CHANGING SCENE

A few months ago a fiery-eyed, long-haired, radical, young postgraduate student stood beside me at a hotel window high over New York. The panorama of the city lay before us. To our right was the magnificent splendor of high-rise office and apartment buildings where some of the world's most affluent citizens work and live. To our left lay one of the nation's most publicized ghettos which stabs the conscience of any American willing to take even a superficial look. The young man beside me was all business. His outstretched hand pointed angrily at the glaring contrast which these polarized life-styles present. His voice was filled with hatred and bitterness as he said, "We're going to burn it down and start all over again."

"What are you going to rebuild in its place?" I asked. He had only illogical answers filled with Marxist cliches.

This was only one of many experiences I have had with radical young student leaders. I have tried to understand their frustration. In fact, I share their frustration when I see injustice on every hand. Deliberately I have visited the slums of our inner cities, attended (incognito) several rock festivals, protest gatherings, and love-ins. I have had innumerable confrontations with activist students on dozens of university and college campuses. I have talked at length with leaders of a variety of factions, and I believe I have acquired a new understanding of the discontented young.

Granting that your world is a bad scene, remember that

my generation also suffered. We came through the Depression and World War II. Hardship and death made us determined that our children would never have to go through another depression or another war. In pursuit of that goal, we chose the wrong means. Instead of turning to spiritual values, we turned to materialism. We collected things, hoarding them against want, constructing an affluent way of life that no one in the world had ever known. Technology burst upon us, and we began to step higher and faster. By the millions, we sent you to colleges and universities. Then we bought you cars and stereos and trips to Europe.

"The future is yours," we finally said. "We're getting tired and it's time for you to take over."

And you threw it all back in our faces.

Astounded and hurt, we asked what you wanted. You said you wanted a world without hunger, without war, without corruption, without hatred, without discrimination, and without pain. And you wanted a world — most of all — without discipline. Agreeing with your dreams, we asked how you would bring about these miracles. Your answers, to this day, have not been very intelligible. And so, throughout this once smiling land, parents and teen-agers began to face each other across millions of dinner tables, glaring or shouting, utterly unable to communicate.

As you pursued your freedom, we saw a spiritual vacuum developing as you turned to cults, drugs, and permissive sex. We did not approve, and most of us still do not understand. But some of us accept by faith your statement that this is your answer to the oppressive materialism that you inherited; that it is the only response you can make to the Establishment's failure to correct its mistakes.

I say there is another alternative which already some of you have understood and grasped. It is faith in Jesus Christ! But more of that presently.

What we who are over thirty have seen clearly is your lack of a viable philosophy on which to build a rewarding life. Because of this lack, we saw how a small band of radical leaders exploited you, and how you swallowed whole bits and pieces of the cant offered to you in university classrooms by radical intellectuals masquerading as college professors.

"Your world is shot through with hypocrisy, hate, imperialism, colonialism, and exploitive capitalism," they taught. "Your heritage is a mess of problems so monstrous that they are beyond solution. That's your birthright, passed on by parents too busy to notice society's garbage. That's your messed-up world. So burn it down. Start all over. Split out and do your own thing."

But is that really the remedy? I think not! Are your problems all that terrible? To be sure, many of them cause the mind to boggle, but take a closer look with me, and perhaps we can find a way to resolve them.

First, there is the staggering social problem of poverty. Looming before that angry grad student and me that day as we gazed across Manhattan was the steeple of a church with a well-publicized multi-million-dollar endowment, while only a few hundred yards away, rat-infested tenements rose where filth, rags, and hunger made a tragic contrast to the stained glass in the church's windows. Our world is full of such inequities, such injustices, and young people do not understand why they are permitted to continue.

While surpluses of food stack up to the skies in North America (grains in the Midwest and citrus fruits in the Southeast and Southwest), exploding populations in underdeveloped countries of Asia, Africa, and South America are getting closer and closer to mass famine. We are told that thousands of people are currently dying from starvation. Says the Stanford biologist, Paul Ehrlich, in headlined articles read around the globe: "There is not the slightest hope of escaping a disastrous time of famines from 1975 onward. It is shockingly apparent that the battle to feed man will end in a rout." A group of 172 eminent people from 19 countries, including 39 Nobel Prize winners and presided over by Sir

Julian Huxley, have petitioned the U.N. to halt the population explosion by every available means short of war. Unless this is accomplished, "there is in prospect a dark age of human misery, famine, and unrest" which will "generate growing panic, exploding into wars fought to appropriate the dwindling means of survival." A careful analyst, Professor L. C. Birch reckons that during the seventies food production will have to be *tripled* to meet the nutritional needs of the world, but we will be fortunate if it can be increased by as little as sixty-five percent and then be equitably distributed.

Very properly, you are concerned, and your compassion is highlighted in *The Greening of America,* the hotly debated book written by Charles A. Reich, professor of law at Yale. "Young people see clearly," he asserts, "a society that is unjust to its poor, its minorities, is run for the benefit of the privileged few, lacks its proclaimed democracy and liberty, is ugly and artificial, destroys the environment and the self. Old people shunted into institutional homes, streets made hideous with commercialism, the competitiveness and sterility of suburban living, the loneliness and anomie of cities, the ruin to nature by bulldozers and pollution, servile conformity, and the artificial quality of plastic lives in plastic homes."[1]

Then, there is the even more complex problem of pollution. Five years ago words like "pollution" were on the fringe of our vocabulary and few of us knew the meaning of "ecology." Today custodians of our natural resources are almost unanimous in warning that unless our atmosphere, waters, and cities are redeemed and cleansed, life on this planet may not survive the seventies, let alone the century.

Millions of youth join Professor Arthur Naftalin of the University of Minnesota, a four-time mayor of Minneapolis, who is disillusioned with our technocratic society, which instead of feeding the world, seems to be retrogressing into the production of pollutants that are about to choke us all to death.

Deep inside us, we sense the ultimate horror of another

kind of pollution. This is that dangling sword of Damocles called *a thermonuclear device.* "The ghostlike character of this development lies in its apparently compulsory trend," reasoned Albert Einstein, one of the fathers of the bomb, adding, "Every step appears as the unavoidable consequence of the preceding one. In the end there beckons, more and more clearly, general annihilation."

You young people who were born into the nuclear age need no convincing that it is a stark and ever present reality. To quote that indefatigable crusader against H-bombs and their kin, the late Bertrand Russell, youth today faces "unyielding despair." While the earth shudders with repeated nuclear tests, modern young people clearly perceive that the human race teeters on the brink of destruction. Whether you like it or not, it is your fate to grow up during one of the most trying times in human history.

This authoritative appraisal of man's hopes for survival comes from the Canadian Peace Research Institute, a panel of intensive researchers. Its head is ex-physicist Dr. Norman Alcook. This distinguished and dedicated scientist, who has thought of little else for ten years than how to avert nuclear engagement, concludes that war is inevitable, that there is not a ray of hope that it can be avoided. When it comes, it will be an all-out, all-destroying war.

Another element of your disenchantment is the so-called generation gap. Unfortunately, it is very real. Many of you, you tell me, are ready to gallop from your pads and communes at any moment, itching to commit any sort of violence that will initiate the revolution.

The older generations are determined to hold you in check. The one ahead of mine digs in to preserve its memories and its moral values. My own, perhaps more conscious of our shortcomings than you may suspect, is grimly committed to averting a cataclysmic blood bath. So the air crackles with potential conflict. And also with the biggest question of our time: Is there any force in the universe that can resolve these pressures and avoid a confrontation?

A few thinkers (in ivory towers) still embrace the hope that man can eventually evolve into a peaceful, prosperous species capable of conducting an orderly society. Few young people buy this. You feel trapped. Ahead, you see the precipice about which Barry McGuire sings in "Eve of Destruction." Your motion pictures repeat the theme. Writer Susan Sontag, commenting on current movies, says that they are all, regardless of nationality, based on the theme of "apocalypse," and that all younger playwrights are completely dedicated to the idea of this ultimate disclosure of God's power.

Finally, the most volatile situation threatening our annihilation is that of racial prejudice and hatred. A famous clergyman has recently stated that we are likely to be exterminated by a racially incited war before the end of this century. Ray Stevens sings desperately that all the children of the world, red and yellow and black and white, are precious in God's sight. "Jesus loves the little children of the world," he chants, but little love seems to be lost between the races at this inflammatory moment of history.

Go with one of my team members, with a reporter, or with a social worker to any American city and you will see the tension between black and white. I had thought a few years ago that our tensions were decreasing. I have changed my mind. Tensions may be increasing, especially in our great Northern cities where people are pressed together, rubbing elbow against elbow. James Meredith, the highly publicized black man from Mississippi, has recently moved back to Mississippi from the North, claiming that the racial situation is much better in the South.

However, the racial problem is not limited to the United States. It is a world-wide phenomenon that illustrates the deep divisions within the human race.

Go to Birmingham, England, and to East London and you will feel the hatred not only between black and white, but among white, black, and red. Go to the longest frontier in the world, which joins China to the Soviet Union, and the static of hatred crackles back and forth like streaks of lightning between white Communist and yellow Communist. Go to Malaysia or Indonesia and you will feel brown man and yellow man grinding against each other. Go to Tanzania in Africa and you will feel the animosity of black against yellow and brown. Or, go to Guyana in South America and you will find black and red pitted against each other.

Even within races there are bitter ethnic, political, and religious hatreds, all emitting sparks which a little fanning can ignite into a conflagration. Go to the Middle East and it is Arab against Israeli; to Ireland and it is Catholic against Protestant; to Cyprus and it is Greek against Turk; to Canada and it is Quebecois against Anglo-Saxon; to South Central Asia and it is Hindu Indian against Moslem Pakistani; to Belgium and it is Walloon against Flem; to Berlin and it is West German against East German.

Arnold Toynbee, the British historian who has studied every world civilization, soberly cautions that "the present world-wide discontent and unrest will become more acute and will express itself in worse and worse outbreaks of violence. In fact," he says, "I would expect to see local civil wars take the place of a third world war."

Under these conditions can the young expect to enjoy a secure life? Recently, I talked to the prime minister of an European country. We were discussing the future of the world, particularly Europe. He said, "The problems we face seem insoluble. I am not sure we have much of a future." Buckminster Fuller, the distinguished futurist, says we have less than a generation in which to clean up our global mess. I say we have less, maybe a decade. An editorial in a London newspaper says: "New York City may be ungovernable." Another editorial says: "America is coming unglued."

Our last three presidents — President Kennedy, President Johnson, and President Nixon — have warned in speech after speech of the dangers that lie ahead for the future generation unless we can somehow resolve our problems.

President Kennedy said: "No man entering upon this office

can fail to be staggered by the enormity of the trials through which we must pass in the next few years and *time is not on our side.*"

Why is man so perverse? I believe it is because he is afflicted with a spiritual disease called "sin" and cannot act rationally long enough to save himself. A British prime minister commented that man's ultimate terror is not really the H-bomb but the human heart. "War was in his heart," said the ancient psalmist (Psalm 55:21).

Leighton Ford relevantly asks, "What is wrong with the world when on the same day our newspapers carried front-page stories of man's first flight into space and of the trial of a man in Israel for his part in the murder of millions of Jews? What is wrong with the world when promises are not enough and we must have contracts; when doors are not enough and we need locks; when laws are not enough and we need police. What is wrong with the world when education has dispelled so much ignorance and raised the literacy rate, yet the worst wars in history have been fought by the most literate nations? What is wrong with the world when government and labor and business produce an affluent society but cannot cope with the spiraling rate of crime, suicide, drug addiction, and moral breakdown?"[2] Such accusations don't tell the whole story, but they are true enough to hurt and to make us wonder if we have become hopelessly insensitive and inept.

During the days of the Renaissance, Pico della Mirandola wrote that man is the most marvelous thing ever seen upon the stage of the world. What has happened to that man? He stands in ruins, it seems, surrounded by the artifacts of his brilliant competence. He is cursed with a flaw, a defect in his make-up, so that whatever he undertakes to do, he succeeds only in corrupting. He progresses upward and downward at the same time. He invents gunpowder only to shoot himself. He invents the airplane and then bombs himself. He invents the thermonuclear warhead which now is poised to exterminate him.

Essentially man is the same today as at the dawn of history when "God saw that the wickedness of man was great in the earth, and that every imagination of the thoughts of his heart was only evil continually" (Genesis 6:5). Karl Marx defined man as a producing animal but never recognized him as morally afflicted, filled with greed, lust, and hatred. This is the fatal flaw of the communist system, as it is of the capitalist system. *The reason man sins is that he is never content to be man; he wants to be God.*

The tragedy of our times is that we have used up all of our options and the questions basic to life which you are asking are not being answered. This is because life's fundamental problems are theological. Modern education is virtually silent. Our educational establishment has been brainwashed into thinking that its job is to educate the mind and build the body but to leave untouched the deeper questions which are essentially spiritual. Some professors venture to say honestly, "We don't know." Only a small minority of Biblically oriented professors and their students are providing authoritative answers. Happily, their number is beginning to grow.

Unfortunately, millions have already joined the Army of Despair, agreeing with Hannah Arendt, the political philosopher, that "The country seems to have fallen under a spell and nothing seems to work anymore. I am very pessimistic."

An engineering student told me, "I feel like a ship at sea without a rudder during a hurricane." Where is there a safe anchorage for this student? Where is your safe haven at this critical time of life when you seek true values and authoritative answers? Lacking a sense of settled purpose or a grasp of the meaning of things, your emotions are apt to run riot. One day you feel that you can lick the world, but the next day you plummet to the depths. No wonder the psychiatrists are overworked. I think I understand: though the pressures of my generation were great, yours are greater.

As you well know, your condition bears a name. You

don't like to hear it because it smacks of immaturity, which you resent. Psychiatrists call it adolescence. Its characteristics are boiling emotions, mercurial moods, and frequent attacks of frustration. It comes, experts say, from today's requirement that your brains be stuffed with knowledge for about ten years more than was formerly the case. In the medieval world, young people became full-fledged citizens in their early teens. Of this violation of nature, I shall have much to say in the chapter entitled "The Sex Hang-up."

If you are from fifteen to twenty-two years old — the U.S. Census reports that you now number over thirty million — you are probably still wrapped in educational swaddling clothes and taking subjects under the general heading of "preparation for life." The trouble is: you believe you *are* ready for life.

Ideals? You have bales of them. You see men dying in wars around the world. You see crime, disease, and violence in cities, suburbia, and country. You see diseases unhealed and hunger unsatisfied. Why? you ask. And no one answers! Already, many of you have moved from what Professor Reich of Yale calls Consciousness I and Consciousness II into the state of consciousness he calls Consciousness III. Consciousness III people are determined to build a better world. [3]

But you are powerless, as you soon discover. You are shackled by financial, social, and familial checkreins.

What of your elders, your "models," to use the psychological designation? Among the adults you know, you find few guiding principles that you can adopt, and this is confusing and infuriating. You require a firm foundation. You seek a positive goal. Given it, your intuition tells you that you may have a chance to fulfill your destiny.

I see that you are impatient, and I do not counsel patience. I see that you are angry, but I do not urge calm. Those qualities are priceless in support of the right cause. Instead, I ask that you read through these next chapters and borrow from them the formula that has changed millions of lives.

I say that you will have your chance to change the world.

I say that you can succeed in your dreams. I pray that you will succeed as no other generation in history has succeeded for several reasons:

Because you have a better education.

Because you are brighter than earlier generations.

Because you are healthier and will live longer.

Because you and your friends — by the thousands — are discovering Jesus Christ.

When I was your age, I felt almost exactly as you do. As a teen-ager, I had a rebellious heart and mind, too.

I lived on a farm in North Carolina where I was the oldest son in a devout Presbyterian family. Each morning I was required to milk ten to twenty dairy cows before breakfast, and I had to attend every worship service conducted at the Presbyterian church to which my parents belonged. I secretly rebelled against both.

My scene was the farm but my "thing" was baseball and girls. My idea of a really cool evening was racing along in my father's car with a pretty girl at my side.

I loved. I hated. I walked on clouds. I groveled in despair. I had all the youthful hang-ups. My world at times seemed to be falling apart. The Great Depression of the thirties was on. Hitler was on the march across Europe. Ethiopia had fallen to Mussolini. Manchuria had been invaded. A few "ridiculous" people were predicting a second world war, but most "experts" were certain that things would work out and that the world was in for a long era of peace. Hundreds of thousands of unemployed people walked the streets looking for work. The heads of families sold apples on street corners. I understood little and resented my parents, my teachers, my humdrum life as a farmhand and high-school student.

Finally I got it all together. In my late adolescence I made a decision, and there followed the experience that changed my life, that filled my future with purpose, fulfillment, meaning, and joy. Since then, I have lived through the Great Depression, World War II, and am now living in the midst of the youth revolution. I have a joy and a peace. Whatever my circumstances, I am convinced beyond the shadow of a doubt that when I received Jesus Christ as my Lord and Savior, I found the secret of life!

Thousands of young people have made this same decision. By following up hundreds of them, and by watching them grow, I have become convinced of their permanent transformation. In future chapters I shall show you how Jesus Christ wants to do the same for you. Give Him a chance — it must be *your* decision — and He will turn your imperfect, adolescent scene into one so great and so high that you will never again settle for less.

2
THE GENERATION GAP

There has always been a gap between the generations — and there always will be. I rather expect it was meant to be. It is normal and wholesome and good when the young are taught to respect age, and when the older generation, assuming the responsibilities that come with age and experience and wisdom, understand the young and guide and support them without stifling.

When this gap is distorted, blown up out of proportion, and even misused, it becomes an unhealthy and abnormal situation.

This is what is happening today.

In the sixties and early seventies the biggest generation bomb in history dropped, detonated, and the explosion gouged a crater which was officially named: the generation gap. Before the fallout was over, sociologists, psychologists, psychiatrists, and statisticians were analyzing, studying, and dissecting both generations. The modern generation gap affected virtually every part of the world. No country, not even China and Russia, was immune. Antipathies heightened and tensions sharpened, until a near life-and-death struggle developed between the old and the young. In Red China, the youth turned in almost total rebellion against the older generation. The same was true in many parts of Europe.

While the impact in America has been less than in some parts of the world, it is greater than in others. It became the straights versus the swingers, the moral versus the permissive, drawn along chronological lines. With short fuses and low boiling points, the generations could, with little warning and less provocation, be expected to split into two irritable and often angry camps, with the smallest of issues taking on enough significance to trigger an argument, a fight, or even a revolution.

Writing in *Look*, Ira Mothmer described the battle lines: "If a number of adults see long hair and not the kids under it . . . then the system starts to break down. Long-hair defensiveness turns to . . . arrogance, and adults anticipate rudeness. The youngsters expect to be put down and reach out for their rights. The town answers with a law when no law was ever needed before, and the scene is set for confrontation."

To assert their distinctiveness more and more, girls wore their hair straight, painted their lips leprosy white, swept their hair across their faces, and circled their eyes with black. Some of the boys angered their parents deliberately with shoulder-length hair. They shunned the shower, on the premise that the older generation had sacrificially institutionalized it on the supposed Biblicism that "cleanliness is next to godliness," and set out to knock down all the tidy blocks that their elders had built up into their carefully constructed parental pyramid. Though this type of teen-ager was still a minority in the late sixties, he was a growing minority.

F. Bronkowski observes: "The generation gap is now a moral chasm across which the young stare at their elders with distrust, convinced that the values that make for success are fakes."[1] So characteristic of our times is the generation gap that Erich Segal built it into the plot of *Love Story*. This work topped the fiction best seller list week after week. Charles Reich's *The Greening of America*, which during those same weeks topped the non-fiction list, deals with the issues which this gap raises. Nor, as I have already mentioned, is the gap an American phenomenon. It peaked enough in China to magnetize twenty-five million Red Guards into a

youth march of unprecedented proportions. In Soviet Russia
an indication of its power is the way it elicits from the pen
of young poet Yeugeny Yevtushenko the widely disseminated
lines:

> I wish to quarrel in a big way,
> My own strength intoxicates me.
> I drive on, plain-speaking, irreconcilable,
> And that means — I am young!

"Send your son to Moscow and he will return an anti-
Communist," observes Felix Houphouet-Boigny, President
of the Ivory Coast. "Send him to the Sorbonne in Paris and
he will return a Communist." The generation gap is as
clearly universal as it is deeply entrenched.

What nettles many young people is the persistent refusal
of their elders to bend to the winds of change, winds which
at times they themselves have blown up. This makes the
youth feel that they are unique — a special electric body who
stand apart from any race of people who have ever inhabited
this planet. This claim to uniqueness has been flung into the
teeth of parents and school administrators around the world.
"If you don't understand, get out of the way," has become
more of a threat than a plea.

The young are right, at least partially, when they indict
the older generation: "It's you adults who push drugs on
us, who print and sell pornography to seize our dimes and
dollars, and your constant barrage of ads pressure us into
taking up habits we would be better without. You open
charge accounts for us to buy a lot of junk we don't need."

I recall reading of a challenge hurled into the teeth of a
middle-aged, suburban father who directed a moderate-sized
industrial empire and, from outward appearances, had it
made. After moodily absorbing a lecture on suburban morality, his son said: "Look at yourself, needing a couple of stiff
drinks before you have the courage to talk with another
human being. Look at you, making it with your neighbor's
wife on the sly just to try to prove that you're really alive.
Look at you, hooked on your cafeteria of pills, making up

dirty names for anybody who isn't in your bag, and messing up the land, the water, and the air for profit and calling this 'nowhere scene' the Great Society. And you're trying to tell me how to live? C'mon, man, you've got to be kidding."

"This is not an easy time to be a father or a mother," *Newsweek* explains. An article on "America, the Modern Byzantium" describes how American youth in their concerted search for new social, sexual, and spiritual plateaus are bent on denying their parents.

Student dissent, no matter from what vantage point one looks at it, has provoked millions of Americans into a state of fury and militant determination to put it down. Rioting students are not a pretty sight, no matter if they are only a tiny minority. Their ribald obscenities and flaming torches have obstructed and upset so many people that parts of the two generations seem to be engaged in a hate match. Young radicals rampaging with bull horns, bludgeoning and abusing their elders who gave them birth — and a heritage of opportunity and freedom such as the world has never seen — have incensed more older people than were angry at Hitler a generation ago.

A counterpunching, fed-up professor of history at the University of Montana, forty-nine-year-old K. Ross Toole, issued a statement that echoed so many adult resentments that it was reprinted in many publications.

He said in part: "I'm a liberal square, and I'm sick of the younger generation's hippies, yippies, militants, and nonsense.

"I am the father of seven children. . . . I am tired of being blamed, maimed, and contrite. I am sick of the total irrationality of the campus rebel whose bearded visage, dirty hair, body odor, and 'tactics' are brutal, naive but dangerous, and the essence of arrogant tyranny — the tyranny of spoiled brats."

Warming to his subject, the professor added: "Every generation has made mistakes and always will. We have made our share. But my generation has made America the most affluent country on earth. It has tackled, head on, a racial problem which no nation on earth in the history of mankind has dared to do. It has publicly declared war on poverty and it has gone to the moon. It has desegregated schools and abolished polio. It has presided over the beginning of what is probably the greatest social and economic revolution in man's history. It has begun these things but not finished them. It has declared itself, committed itself, taxed itself, and run itself into the ground in the cause of social justice and reform."

He offered ideas with which a vast majority of both generations agreed. For example: "Society hangs together by the stitching of many threads. No eighteen-year-old simply is the product of his eighteen years. He is the product of 3,000 years of the development of mankind, and throughout these years injustice has existed and been fought; rules have grown outmoded and been changed; doom has hung over men and been avoided; unjust wars have occurred; pain has been the cost of progress — and man has persevered."

Which brings up the matter of where the generation gap came from. What we are seeing today is not new in history. But it has become more concentrated and more intense.

There have been dramatic confrontations between the generations before in history. For example, we are deeply concerned about campus violence. "What's happening to our children?" parents wonder, adding, "When I was in school, we played pranks, but it was nothing like this!" Our own history provides an answer. Young Americans have always been rather violent. Many a riot disrupted Yankee campuses when our land was young.

According to *Time*, a Harvard professor named Eliphalet Pearsons kept a diary. One 1788 entry said: "In the hall at breakfast this morning, bisket, tea, cups, saucers, and a knife were thrown at tutors. At even prayers the lights were all extinguished by powder and lead." *Time* goes on: "Other U.S. college casualties included one undergraduate dead in a duel at South Carolina College and another at Dickinson, several students shot at Ohio's Miami University, a professor killed at the University of Virginia, and the President of Mississippi's Oakland College stabbed to death by a student." Human nature has not changed. As in Noah's day, so today: "the Lord said . . . the imagination of man's heart is evil from his youth" (Genesis 8:21).

Today we are much concerned about the casual way in which some of our children vanish from home, taking to the highways in search of independence and a taste of reality. Thousands of young people run away each year, and adults, not understanding the phenomenon, take each departure as if it was unprecedented. But running away from home is an ancient dodge.

A few years ago *Time* published an essay entitled "On Losing One's Cool About the Young." It made these points: "Before the industrial revolution, youth could hardly be said to exist at all. Medieval artists even seemed ignorant of what a child looked like. A twelfth century miniature illustrating Jesus' injunction to 'suffer the little children to come unto me' shows Christ surrounded by eight undersized men. Before the seventeenth century, a child passed directly into the adult world between the ages of five and seven." In the few schools that existed, pupils "carried weapons which they were supposed to check at the schoolroom door."

Then came the industrial revolution and the establishment of factories. Farmers left their land to work in cities. Their children roamed the streets, causing all kinds of trouble and upsetting adult sensibilities so severely that the British House of Commons passed the first law to establish day schools, which they hoped would control and train young people for the work force required by the new machine age. The arrangements succeeded. The troublemaker of the alleyways turned into a schoolboy, gaining status and respectability. Instead of being a prime candidate for delinquency, he became a person to be cultivated and nourished with the best instruction his parents could afford. So the child-centered home was born.

In the United States, as the nation expanded and prospered, families concentrated their hopes more and more in their young people, giving them every encouragement to grow into successful citizens. The young, flattered by their new role and knowing that they would graduate presently into a gratifying life-style, accepted these attentions and asked for more. The system worked well, turning out workers and citizens by the millions.

At the turn of the century it seemed that science and education were about to create the perfect society. As a matter of fact, in 1900 nearly all the predictions by intellectuals, writers, political leaders, and diplomats were heralding a century of peace and justice. A new magazine was founded in America called *The Christian Century*. The twentieth century was to have been the Christian century. During this century man was supposed to have perfected himself, eradicated the flaws in his character, solved his problems, ended all wars, and begun to live happily ever after. Theologians were to write, "man has now come of age."

It was too good to last!

Jean Jacques Rousseau had already exploded the dream with a devastating attack on the new machine age. Suddenly his anti-materialistic philosophy was toasted everywhere. A machine-age man was a nincompoop compared to the untutored but noble savage, said Rousseau. Life was not meant to be a regimented parade of service to machines; it was meant to be *lived* in the service of one's senses. The young were to be educated, not through their brains but through their sensations. Nature, not society, was the wiser schoolmaster.

With mentors like that, who needed God? Man was self-fulfilling and self-perfecting. Both young people and adults believed it. A policy of laissez-faire invaded the home. Permissiveness began to take over education. Rousseau's freewheeling philosophy spread like a prairie fire across Europe and into the United States. "Keep your child's mind idle as long as you can," he directed. Other philosophers of the nineteenth century, such as Hegel and Nietzsche, were making their impact. Dewey was beginning to teach his behaviorism at Columbia — and Dr. Spock was on the horizon.

Their fantasy finally exploded in the blood bath of World War I. As millions of young men died "to save the world for democracy," and as it became obvious that another dream had been a mirage, young people turned bitter, realizing they had been disillusioned. Their goal became mindless, a search for pleasure through the senses a la Rousseau! They embraced the teachings of Sigmund Freud.

Freud said that tensions stored too long in the subconscious became explosive. War was man's outlet for his repressed anger. Youth decided that the remedy for hatred and violence was to take another road. Be open, be frank, and liberate the id. Clearly the trouble with mankind, they said, was his lack of sexual freedom. College flappers shortened their skirts and took on the "flat" look. The heroes of F. Scott Fitzgerald set a "follow me" pattern. It was the jazz age and it lasted until the Depression of 1929.

When Wall Street cracked wide open, family purses were emptied. For the first time in years families drew together, trying to weather the economic typhoon. Suddenly mere survival became the whole purpose of living. The generation gap almost disappeared — out of necessity! As the Harvard sociologist, Seymour Martin Lipset, points out, "The authority of parents and teachers, which was weak in the twenties, came back in the thirties because students were more dependent on them."[2]

My own family on a farm in North Carolina lost almost everything. My father's life savings were lost in a bank closure. All of us children joined our father and mother in helping to make a living. We all faced the same challenges and made the same sacrifices.

Finally, the tide turned. Fathers and mothers went back to work, determined that their children should never suffer similar privations. It was a noble objective, but their drive for security became diverted into a passion for possessions.

Soon their children, in college and out, became the most pampered generation in the world's history. By the 1960s the United States had a new ruling class — the teen-ager!

Recognizing that you young people have had to cope with having been reared in a different culture with different standards and different pressures comes hard to most of us adults. Sherman B. Chickering, the twenty-seven-year-old editor of *Moderator* magazine, adds another dimension: "Ours was an Oepidal childhood, especially if we were war babies," he says. "The father was away and the mother worked. Postwar conditions did not change too much. Our mothers were dominant figures in our lives because our fathers were so involved in 'making it' . . . their children, especially the boys, became uprooted. Boys tended to identify more with the 'emotional' qualities of their mothers rather than the principles and practices of their fathers."

Of the effect of television, he says: "Both content and medium conspired to make us more sophisticated than any amount of heritage, tutelage, or erudition could have. . . . We learned to see right through to the quick . . . the media made hypocrites, squares, finks, and fiends of the world's big shots, and made hippies and swingers of us little boys."

As for the discipline and help traditionally supplied by a boy's dad, he says: "Father was not to be listened to for advice on the big questions later on because he didn't bother with the little questions earlier."

So young people began to judge their elders. Something was wrong if the nation's adult leadership could not devise a program for peace. As students were drafted, served their time, and returned to tell stories of incomprehensible military hang-ups, the discontent spread. Thousands of youth became involved in the racial struggle of the sixties and aligned themselves with leaders like Martin Luther King and Whitney Young. While the revolution made great strides, for many it was not fast enough. Vitally concerned student groups passed resolutions and worked in political campaigns, but to no avail. They were shocked and humiliated to discover their powerlessness. The experience sent some of them into raging vendettas against "the establishment." The Communists had a field day behind scores of "fronts." Radicalism arose. Violence spread.

And so appeared the great generation gulf: fixed — but how fixed it would remain was something yet to be seen. From the point of view of many parents it was a fulfillment of the Biblical prediction: "In the last days" youth would be "without any regard for what their parents taught them."

And as we think about why the generation gap has opened up so inscrutably, right here lies a reason. Since education began, the elders taught the youngsters. But this has changed dramatically. "Generation gap, step aside for the 'education gap,'" suggested *Time* magazine early in 1971: "According to a study based on the census, the chief reason for conflict between parents and children may well be their sharply changing exposures to learning. The proportion of young adults with high school diplomas has risen from 30% in 1940 to 75% today; those with one or more years of college have increased from 13% to 31%, and college degree holders have almost tripled, from 6% to 16%. By contrast, the fathers of nearly two-thirds of today's college students did not go beyond high school."

The situation is reversing itself. Buckminster Fuller says, "Approximately everything man thought he understood will be useless within the next decade." The time is coming soon, he believes, when *children will be teaching their parents.* "The Bible was right," he adds, when it predicted that a "child shall lead them." This fact is overwhelming and incomprehensible to the elders, but often taken for granted by the heady generation of youth, who see knowledge double every fifteen years and are surrounded by seventy-five percent of the scientists of history, most of them young. And while the young are geniuses at laying claim to the new stockpiles of facts at man's command, they are comparably adept at laying the blame for pollution, poverty, and proliferating thermonuclear weaponry at the feet of their forebears.

Not only are education and technology wedges widening the generation gap, but so is the thing which makes it possible — opulence. John Leo, writing in *The Christian Herald*, points to the youth counter-culture having been "born of affluence, mobility, and prolonged adolescence. A society that keeps its young out of approved adult roles until the age of twenty-one or twenty-two, produces children at a rate that makes them half the population, and then supplies them with enough money to create and respond to its own economic markets, is doing nothing less than spawning a new culture. Stripped of technical jargon, what the social scientists have been telling us is that young people, formerly oriented toward family and tradition, are now oriented toward one another." Possibly there is at present a slight shift back in this area. *Time* analyzes in a cover story, "The Cooling of America," that as we have come through a recession at the beginning of the seventies, it is obvious that this in itself has been at least a slight healing balm on the generation wound.

Causes of the generation rift could be summed up, in addition to the foregoing, as: the natural rebellion of the human heart; the emptiness evident everywhere; the constant erosion and dehumanization of personality by a machine-oriented age; the lack of purpose and meaning; the tragic failure of our educational system which seems more and more to alienate the young and consequently anger their parents; the overriding social problems that have no foreseeable solutions; the failure of parents to live what they preach; the failure of government to understand that the basic gut-level problems facing the nation are not materialistic and social, but moral and spiritual.

The church, too, is at fault in turning from Biblical proclamation to social and political activism. Too many clergy are just plain phonies in the eyes of the youth. They want to see discipleship in the lives of their parents and they want the clergy to "tell it like it is" from the pulpit. How long will it take to learn that God meant it when He warned, "The nation which will not serve me shall perish"? How long will it take to learn that astronomical congressional appropriations are no substitute for spiritual awakening, which, in the final analysis, alone can reform our institutions and the individuals who make up society?

In searching for ways to bridge the generation gap, there is no doubt that we, as parents, are going to have to practice what we preach by striving more and more to bring our conduct into line with our code of beliefs. No mother can demand that her daughter abstain from sleeping around when she herself is flirting and on occasion compromising her own moral conduct. No father, who wavers between heavy social drinking and occasional binges to the edge of alcoholism, and who can't speak a pleasant word in the morning until he has had a cigarette, can yell incessantly at his son to get off marijuana, the route that often leads to hard drugs. Consistency, constancy, and undeviating diligence to maintain Christian character are a must if the older generation is to command respect or even a hearing from the young.

Another point for parents: There are times when our lives are straight as a gun barrel, but instead of letting our children be placed in the hands of God by prayer, to be developed by Him into their unique potential, we try to force them into a mold. "Be not angry that you cannot make others as you wish them to be, since you cannot make yourself as you wish to be" (Thomas à Kempis).

Soon after I was converted, I left the farm in North Carolina and went to school in Florida and later went to college near Chicago. At the end of World War II I joined Youth for Christ International as their first full-time evangelist. When I went home to see my folks on the farm in North Carolina, I probably appeared "far out." I was smartly dressed, and my outfit included a colorful, hand-painted bow tie. My attire was certainly not conventional clerical garb, and I am sure my family was rather embarrassed to see me stand in the pulpit in such clothes.

The younger generation doesn't want to be a rubber stamp of its elders. "A chip off the old block" is a phrase which would not appear in a youth dictionary.

In the past we have required our young to defer significant feats both great and small, to be content with contests for grades and athletic letters, and to keep their heads buried in their books. So the average student, full-grown and exploding with energy, remains a dependent whose actions are monitored and whose life is carefully protected by his elders. As the years pass he grows increasingly restive, knowing himself to be an adult with a large stock of relevant knowledge, though with less experience than his parents, but often treated like a child. Today his universal rejection of this role is exploited by the radicals who have founded "the movement." It is international in scope, and it is passionate in commitment.

But there is another side to the coin. Many times young people reject their parents for no reason at all. Many parents have done a good job rearing their children. Showering their children with love, they have spent hours every week with them. They have prayed earnestly for them and sacrificed much for them. Then when their children reach a certain age, they reject their parents. As Erich Segal put it: "I would define a father as a person who will someday be misunderstood by his son." One of life's most painful experiences is for a parent to be rejected by his child. This is happening more and more in our society. Often it is not the parent's fault — it is the child's fault. There is a certain indefinable age in the early teens at which God treats a child as an adult. Then he must make his own moral decisions.

In concluding this chapter, I am going to say something which many of the older generation will not agree with, but which I have felt for a long time. Charles Reich is right in *The Greening of America*, and Bob Dylan, the Beatles, and the Byrds in their lyrics, when they refer to a world being raped, robbed, and ripped off in a manner which litters our countrysides and renders our cities ugly and in parts uninhabitable. They point out the kind of treadmill, threadbare, plastic lives which too many millions of people are living in order to hang in there: in the business rat race; in keeping up with the Joneses socially or the brain-heads intellectually. Life is much more than a tussle to come out top dog.

Reich is especially apt in his analysis of Consciousness I (granddad, the American Medical Association, pioneers); Consciousness II (where the mad, racing modern is: the button-down liberal; the passionate do-gooder and the institutional man); Consciousness III (the new sensibility of the Aquarian Age). III believes in the integrity of the here and now. III believes in work as pleasure, as craftsmanship. III believes in instinct, mystery, joy, accidents, adventures. III wears liberated costumes, not for parade but for sheer comfort. III does not judge; III accepts. III shares rather than merely competes. III people love each other. III people are not ashamed to weep and to laugh only when they feel like it. [3]

This is where the generations can meet. But the simple, eager life of Consciousness III can only be realized by both generations if we are prepared to include the fifth dimension, the vertical relationship of man with God — call it Consciousness IV if you will. Jesus taught precisely these same values — here and now values because of *THERE* and *THEN* values. He bade the rich young ruler, a Consciousness II man, to sell out, leave all, and follow Him. If he did, in the here and now Kingdom of God he would receive "very much more in this present life — and eternal life in the world to come." Jesus told another Consciousness II man, Nicodemus, that if he was to enter this Kingdom of God — Consciousness IV — he "must be born again."

Jesus taught that the highest consciousness is the Holy Spirit-inspired consciousness that we have been regenerated:

that is, born from above. Regeneration would make work a pleasure — "Whatsoever ye do in word or deed, do all to the glory of God." Consciousness IV — in Christ — brings mystery: "Great is the mystery of godliness"; brings joy: "that your joy may be full"; brings liberation: "whom the Son sets free he is free indeed"; does not judge: "judge not that ye be not judged"; shares: "bear ye one another's burdens"; brings love: "by this shall all men know that ye are my disciples, because ye have love one to another"; is not ashamed to weep: "Jesus wept."

Yes, the greening of America, the greening of the world, which will happen to the valley separating the generations, is indeed possible if we will receive: "The Lord is my shepherd; I shall not want. . . . He leadeth me . . . in green pastures."

John Lennon entered 1971 with the awareness: "The dream is over. I'm not just talking about the generation thing. It's over and we gotta — I've personally gotta — get down to so-called reality."

Reality, the real thing, Consciousness IV, can be had by accepting Jesus Christ, the Son of God, as Savior and Lord. Dollar-power or flower-power people: let us open our hearts to the Son of God as a flower opens to the sun in the morning.

3
HANG-UPS

The dictionary defines hang-up as an "inhibition." Today it means that and more. Something like a psychological or emotional snag. Nobody seems to know where the expression came from, but everyone knows what it means.

Almost everyone has a hang-up of some sort. Young people come up to me and say, "Dr. Graham, I've got a hang-up. What can I do about it?"

I tell them about Absalom. Absalom was a young man with a hang-up, and his story is told in the Bible. He was handsome. He had long hair. He rebelled against his father. He ran away from home. His name meant "father of peace," but not once in his life did he live up to it. Though he was part of the Establishment (his father was King David), he was opposed to it. He hated the military. He crusaded for social justice, but for selfish reasons. He tried to start a revolution that would overthrow the old order.

Like many modern youths, he always seemed to be trying to find out who he was. A psychiatrist of the twentieth century would say, "Man, you're up to your ears in an identity crisis." He fell in and out of "religion" (as well as love) a half-dozen times. In the end, he got hung up by his long hair in an oak tree.

Whoever said that history never repeats itself did not know about Absalom. He was almost an exact replica of some of today's young people.

If you are like most young persons, you have an average

allotment of youthful hang-ups. Normally you will resolve some of them and compound others. Reacting to pressures from outside and inside your body, you may rebel and demonstrate. And then you will wonder, to what end? The world remains much as it was. At times you may want to hide from everyone. At times, you may want to smash things. Tedd Smith, our crusade pianist, has written a piano solo entitled "Smash and Grab World." It is a symbol of our times.

Absalom apparently had a *hang-up about his hair* long before he got hung up by it. He visited the barber once a year, and when he got there, the Bible says, he would have accumulated six and a quarter pounds of hair. We read that "in all Israel there was none to be so much praised as Absalom for his beauty" (2 Samuel 14:25). People would instinctively turn and look at him when he walked by — some with envy, most with admiration.

Times change. When I was a child, I could hardly wait to grow up so I could shave. Today a boy can hardly wait to grow a beard. I have noticed that middle-aged men now wear long hair and so do some older people. Even some football players look like Absaloms. But young people must look different, so many of them have shaved their heads and call themselves "skinheads."

For Absalom, this matter of the *identity crisis* was a real hang-up. Who was he? Was he a mouse, a man, or a god? Did he want human rights or the divine right of kings? Or neither? Or both? Was he born to be a king or a prince in permanent exile? Or a fatalistic loser? Was his real self a sexual, a social, or a spiritual being? He never seemed to know. He never graduated from being a mixed-up kid. His father David had once asked, as had Moses before him, "Who am I?" Moses and David found out. Absalom never developed this sense of belonging. To him, "Who am I?" remained a permanent enigma. He was like Edward Dahlberg, the writer who had observed: "At nineteen I was a stranger to myself. At forty I asked, 'Who am I?' At fifty I concluded I would never know."

This unexplored personal wilderness is the home of millions of young people. Ninety-two percent of all Canadian university students, according to June Callwood, the Toronto sociologist, don't really know who they are.

The Bible says that man is an immortal soul. When God made man in the first place, He created him and "breathed into his nostrils the breath of life; and man became a living soul" (Genesis 2:7). One's soul is the essence, the core, the eternal and real person. And he will be restless until he opens his life to Jesus Christ as Savior and Lord.

"Why art thou cast down, O my soul? And why art thou disquieted within me?" asked Absalom's father, David, and he also had the answer, which it appears Absalom never had.

Youth can find total "soul fulfillment" when they believe with their heads and their hearts in Jesus Christ as Savior and Lord. Only He can totally satisfy and give purpose and meaning to life. He solves the identity crisis.

Another hang-up which the modern youth has in common with Absalom *is his father*. Many parents today are under vitriolic attack by their children. I have heard a hippie defined as someone who loves everyone except his parents.

In all history there has never been a human father who loved his son as David loved Absalom. Time after time David tried to communicate with him and was repulsed.

Even when Absalom was leading an insurrection against the state, David gave an order to his military leaders: "Deal gently for my sake . . . with Absalom" (2 Samuel 18:5).

In the thick of the battle we read that a heartbroken David "longed to go forth unto Absalom" (2 Samuel 13:39). To his father's heart, Absalom's behavior was absolutely incomprehensible. "My son, which I have brought forth, seeketh my life," he lamented. When the battle thickened and it seemed that Absalom would be defeated, David's first question was, "Is the young man safe?"

Finally, when Absalom was slain, contrary to orders, and word reached the king, we read that David locked himself in his room, mourning and weeping in a loud voice: "O my son Absalom, my son, my son Absalom! would God I had died for thee, O Absalom, my son, my son!" (2 Samuel 18: 33).

Jesus tells of a son who got hung up on home and took a journey into a far-off country. Throughout the world today, tens of thousands of youths get bugged with home life and find domestic routines a drag. So they leave home. The Beatles wrote a song about "Leaving Home." It is part of the restlessness of our times. Of course there comes a day when a youth is supposed to leave home. When he is married, the Bible even commands: "Therefore shall a man leave his father and his mother, and shall cleave unto his wife: and they shall be one flesh" (Genesis 2:24). To be sure, some young people stay around home too long after they have assumed responsibility for their own family, and this stunts development and independence. On the other hand, too many have left in search of excitement and pleasure, thinking to find happiness in the bright lights of the city, only to discover frustration and emptiness worse than anything experienced before. How many young girls in our big cities now are crying themselves to sleep at night and wishing they could swallow their pride and go back home to father and mother? Many families have a boy or girl who has left with no forwarding address and, like David, they weep for their prodigals every day.

Absalom had a *hang-up about sex.* For Absalom, sex was for personal pleasure. The Bible does not teach that sex is sin, but it does teach that the wrong use of sex is sin. Without sex none of us would be here. God ordained and blessed sex but only within the confines of marriage. But what made Absalom's hang-up over sex so much like that of many young people today is that he engaged in it as an open exhibition. We read that he went "upon the top of the house; and Absalom" engaged in public immorality with ten women "in the sight of all Israel" (2 Samuel 16:22). There seemed to be no sense of shame in Absalom's immoral display. There was only contempt for his father; but even more serious, contempt for God's law. But Absalom paid for his sin with a stricken conscience and a violent death.

Today the entire atmosphere of our society is saturated with sex. It is almost impossible for a young man or a young woman to resist its pull. Few, outside those who have put their faith in Jesus Christ and have His spiritual resources at their command, can resist this compelling power within us and outside of us. Some of the new sensitivity groups are becoming nothing but sexual orgies in the name of love and understanding.

The Bible says: "Shun the very appearance of evil" and "Flee youthful lusts." Jesus said that looking with lust in your eye produces the act in your heart.

If sex is your hang-up, then give your life to Christ. He can divert this tremendous energy and power that God gave you into constructive channels. I do not believe that anyone can become a dynamic Christian until his sex life is surrendered to God. No man can be a *complete* man apart from the Lordship of Christ, including this area so long identified with masculinity.

Absalom, like millions of young people today, was *hung up on the establishment.* For many years he served in the political system of his time. He had decided to work within the system, and he was a success. The Bible says: "Absalom stole the hearts of the men of Israel" (2 Samuel 15:6). But eventually he became impatient at the slow process of change and got hung up on politics.

Many of you who read these words have tried your hand in political campaigns and you have learned some bitter lessons. Many of you have told me that you feel empty and let down. Either your candidate was not elected, or, if he was, he was not the man you thought he was going to be. Many of you have called politics a bad scene, one that is incapable of producing lasting results.

I have lived long enough now to see the United States taken over by a bureaucratic monster. The monster is no longer responsive to elected officials. It feeds on itself. Even a president can barely make a dent in it. Yet, with all of its faults and failures, the democratic system is still the best method of government in the world. The only alternative is a society organized, built, and held together by force, by a dictator.

Absalom's hang-up made him typical of today's rebel in revolt against the prevailing order, against the institutionalized system which was in power in his day, but without a better alternative. Finally the time came when Absalom decided to try to overthrow the system by violence. Like so many young people today, he had no substitute plan.

When I ask young people what they would put in place of the present American system or the present British system, they look blank. They know the system needs changing. They think that if they tear it down or burn it down, they can do a better job rebuilding it, but they apparently have no plans for rebuilding. I can assure you that after it has been torn down and your generation begins to rebuild, the result will be just as bad because you, too, are filled with lust, greed, hate, prejudice, and all the other sins of which your forefathers were guilty. And it may be worse because of technical and scientific advances, in the sense that a crash in a jet is more disastrous than one in a covered wagon or a Model T.

Many countries of the world may look peaceful and progressive, but they are held together by force. A concentration camp is a place of law and order and "peace." But is that the kind of peace you want? That's the kind of peace you are going to get if you don't determine to work within the system for the changes that are necessary.

Absalom began his subversive plan by charming the people and "rapping" with them. Social justice was the campaign slogan, and he became the champion of the common people of Israel. However, he was not really interested in the common people; he was only interested in self-advancement. Some young people can cry, "More power to the people!" when what some of their leaders really want is more power for themselves.

There was no doubt that Absalom had a case. Things needed changing, but he chose the wrong way to change them. During the past few years many countries have spawned a strange new breed of angry young men and women who burn flags and peddle hate literature about the country which gave them birth. They reject the freedoms presented to them by generations who worked, bled, and died that they might have these freedoms.

There is no doubt that we need social reform. On the other hand, the quest for social betterment is not a unique something about which only the young are concerned. To quote again from Professor K. Ross Toole: "Sensitivity is not the property of the young, nor was it invented in the sixties. The young of any generation have felt the same impulse to grow, to reach out, to touch stars. . . . Young men and young women have always stood on the same hill and felt the same vague sense of restraint that separated them from the ultimate experience."

The professor proposed a solution: "What we need is a reappraisal of our own middle-class selves, our worth and our hard-won progress. We need . . . to assess a weapon we came by the hard way, by travail and labor; from authority, as parents, teachers, businessmen, workers and politicians. . . . This is a country full of concerned people like myself. It is also a country full of people fed up with nonsense. We need — those of us over thirty, tax-ridden, harried, confused, weary and beaten — to reassert our hard-won prerogatives. It is our country, too. We fought for it, bled for it, dreamed for it, and we love it. It is time to reclaim it. The best place to start is at home."

These sentiments from Professor Toole are an expression of a majority of public opinion, both young and old. If success is ever to be realized, our generations must work together and listen to each other, which is one of the first requirements of cooperation.

At this point, the Gospel of Jesus Christ is relevant as the great reconciler. The Apostle John, in his first epistle, declared: "To you, young men, I have written," and "To you fathers, I have written." This is, to the young activists and to the old guard: "It is by this that we know what love is: that Christ laid down his life for us. And we in our turn are bound to lay down our lives for our brothers. But if a man has enough to live on, and yet when he sees his brother in need shuts up his heart against him, how can it be said that the divine love dwells in him? My children, love must not be a matter of words or talk; it must be genuine, and show itself in action. This is how we may know that we belong to the realm of truth" (NEB, 1 John 3:16-19).

Another hang-up which Absalom might have shared with modern youth was *technology.* The Scripture says that his people were those who "went in their simplicity."

The widespread rejection by our youth today of affluence, and of what German youth are calling "soulless materialism," is a sentiment almost universally shared. Pope Paul was so very right when, as Lent 1971 began, he referred to the "disillusioning road that has led us to modern materialism."

America has become the most spectacularly technological nation in history. Gadgetry has become a symbol of our times, as have credit cards, charge accounts, mod shops, boutiques, drag strips and rock music instruments of an infinite variety. Computers run the business world and unbelievable advances are being made in the areas of communication and transportation.

By the time you get through college, communications experts say, you have listened to 350,000 TV commercials. You have spent more hours before the tube than in school, averaging twenty-three or more hours a week. Your freedom of thought has been forfeited largely to robot brains. In the realm of violence, by the time you are fifteen you have seen 15,000 murders on television. You have also seen violence in

Vietnam, the Middle East, Dallas, Los Angeles and Kent State. And you have lived with it in your streets.

"Science has diminished the individual," say J. Robert Moskin. "It has shown man that he lives on an insignificant planet in the suburbs of a not too prominent solar system. . . . It has shown man that his subconscious and the laws of probability control much of his activity and success." [1]

Like Absalom, who was enchanted with simplicity, there is a widespread yearning to rid ourselves of the overweening, all-controlling, liberty-sacrificing technology of our times. Charles Lindbergh was quoted recently as saying that if he had to choose between birds and airplanes, he would choose birds. Joseph Wood Krutch has reminded us that Alexander Graham Bell wouldn't have a telephone in his house. And Vladmir Zworykin, the genius who gave us television, when asked to name his favorite TV program, replied, "None!"

Yet we keep reaching further into inner and outer space, seeking security, but finding that each new penetration makes us less secure. "Our times are symbolized by the airplane," said a Scottish peer to the House of Lords. "If it stops, it falls out of the sky and is destroyed." Sometimes many of us feel that man has begun his descent.

This surfeit of science and near complete control over our lives by technology is strait-jacketing us. So we have tended, in the absence of any other motive, to make a religion out of science. This is now rapidly changing. As we loosen the ancient bonds of gravity, we fall into bondage to nothingness. Consider Norman Mailer's observation: "Nihilism found its perfect expression in the odyssey to the moon — because we went there without knowing why we went." He has a point. We border on the deification of science. Long ago, when science built the Tower of Babel, God sent a judgment. When Nebuchadnezzar built the greatest city in the world and had himself deified, God sent a judgment.

Carl Kaufman, of *Look* magazine, visited the Space Center

at Houston and wrote, "I became increasingly aware that I had come within the fastness of a new religious sect. There were holy places, entry to which was secured only by vari-colored badges designating rank in a complex priesthood." Concluded Kaufman, "The United States, I realized, had at last unveiled a new deity: Technigod! Here was a god of such power and reach that he might hope to unify the world."

This kind of worship almost obsessed America for a while. Much to our credit, we are beginning to put the achievements of science in their proper perspective. We are beginning to realize that man is far more important than the machines he builds. The Second Commandment says: "Thou shalt not take unto thee any graven image." When finely honed instruments or ingenious machines begin to assume the faces of graven gods, we have traveled a long way down the road to idolatry.

Absalom had a hang-up about the *military*. Among the people he detested most was Joab, Commander-in-Chief of Israel's army.

"I hate war," said President Roosevelt a generation ago. "War is hell," lamented General Sherman a century ago. That was before nuclear weapons. I do not wonder that there are sentiments for peace everywhere when we are told about the frightful horror of modern weapons and the possibility of racial genocide.

I can remember when I was a boy, evangelists and preachers would come to town and warn the people of wars and rumors of wars. They warned about the wrath of God to come and about the possibility of the end of the world. The intellectual elite in our community would laugh at them. Newspaper editorials would mock them. This is no longer true. The prophets of doom now are our scientists and sociologists.

The Charter of the United Nations says in its preamble: "We the people determined to save succeeding generations from war." Since that was written, more than fifty wars have been fought. At this moment many little wars that you rarely read about are going on all over the world.

I have to tell it like it is. The Bible teaches that there will be wars and rumors of wars until the end of time. Ezekiel, the prophet, warned: "They have seduced my people, saying, Peace; and there was no peace" (Ezekiel 13:10).

Where does war come from? The Bible asks that question and gives a straight answer: "From whence come wars and fightings among you? come they not hence, even of your lusts?" (James 4:1). In other words, James is saying war comes from the lust within the hearts of men. We shall never have permanent world peace until human nature has been changed and transformed. Until that time, we have to make the best of a bad situation. We must have police to enforce the law. We must have military forces to protect us from aggression.

Absalom had a hang-up about *revolution*. He was a convinced revolutionary and he became an insurrectionist. To execute his revolution, he had to use violence, so Absalom mobilized a motley host of revolutionaries. "And the conspiracy was strong; for the people increased continually with Absalom" (2 Samuel 15:12). One might say that Absalom had a double standard. To him the military complex of Israel was an evil, but at the time of his death, he was leading an uprising to which he brought all the deception, violence and treason he could recruit in order to win. For him, the end justified the means.

A minority of youth today are hung up on a revolution. The Weathermen are typical of a rash of radical organizations, which, while categorically condemning war, have no qualms about blowing up a factory, killing a policeman, or planting a bomb.

I have said that it is sheer hypocrisy for the older generation to ask the young to refrain from getting high on marijuana while they persist in getting stoned on liquor. But I am also convinced that it is equally hypocritical for young radicals to demand that the United States renounce all acts of war while they themselves justify the use of violence to gain their ends. The reason for this inconsistency is that radical youths are hung up on revolution. And revolution can become an enslaving bondage as can any other compulsion.

Jesus Christ was the greatest revolutionary of all times in the truest sense. He so revolutionized lives that after His ascension into Heaven His disciples went throughout the world sharing His message with their contemporaries. Their message was so revolutionary that people said: "These that have turned the world upside down are come hither" (Acts 17:6).

This is why the Jesus revolution is so important: Right now, Jesus is revolutionizing lives throughout the world. He could revolutionize your life right now.

During all the time of his rebellion, Absalom could not escape God. You cannot escape God either.

Just after the student revolt in Paris, Sargent Shriver, who was then the American ambassador, invited me to meet with some French student leaders in his home in Paris. The basic questions I heard during that three-hour discussion are exactly the same as those which my generation was asking before World War II.

And the basic issues went back to the question that a young man asked Jesus two thousand years ago: "What must I do to inherit eternal life?" That young man was seeking happiness, satisfaction, and peace. Today millions of youth are searching for the same things. Some are coming to grips with their inner selves for the first time, and they don't like what they find.

Perhaps you have a totally different hang-up than Absalom had. Jesus Christ hung on the cross in order that God might provide a way to forgive your sins and to help you solve your hang-ups. In Galatians 3:13 the Scripture says: "Cursed is every one that hangeth on a tree." Jesus Christ hung on that tree and, in doing so, assumed all our hang-ups. We can come to that cross by simple faith and have our lives changed, redirected, and revolutionized. All your problems will not be solved immediately, but deep in your heart will be a sense of fulfillment, joy, and peace, and you will be able to face the real world with confidence. You will have new resources at your disposal.

Absalom could not escape from his hang-ups without God — neither can you!

4
BAD VIBRATIONS

Erich Segal, author of *Love Story*, in a recent interview recalled a visit to London where he met the Beatles. "I could see them breaking up while I was there," he recollects. "I saw the bad vibrations."

Everywhere you go today the young are complaining about "bad vibrations." Bad "vibes" have to do with being bored, with feelings of disappointment, depression, frustration, guilt, despair. They are the opposite of harmony, fulfillment, and meaning.

Bad vibrations are the "off-key discords" that make you want to "tune out" that channel. Bad vibrations are the sure provision of God to warn you that you have lost your moorings and are off course; that you cannot sin and get away with it; that "the way of transgressors is hard." Did you ever think of that? That because God is love, and loves you, He has so designed your life that the route to being forever lost is the roughest of all passages? "God is love" means that He tries constantly to block your route to destruction.

Bad vibrations have shaken our youth because in their attempt to run away from God and immunize themselves from His call, they have done things which have blown their minds, burned out their bodies, bombed their emotions, dulled their consciences and crippled their wills. These bad vibrations have also left their souls restless and their hearts crying out for a peace, joy and fulfillment that only God can give.

Bad vibrations come from our sins, and the Bible has a great deal to say about the sins of youth. In Genesis 8 we read that man's "imagination is evil from his youth." Only Christ was immune from the blood poisoning of sin. Every other Biblical personality was infected. In the book of Job, a character complained that "his bones are full of the sin of his youth," and Job himself lamented "the iniquities of my youth." David the king asked of the Lord, "Remember not the sins of my youth." Jeremiah attributed Israel's troubles to the fact that "we and our fathers from our youth have sinned," and pointed to certain of his contemporaries who "have only done evil before the Lord from their youth." Solomon wrote of the young woman "which forsaketh the guide of her youth" and flings her purity to the winds. The priest Eli died of a broken heart upon hearing the report of his immoral sons: "The sin of the young men was very great."

Paul cautioned Timothy, a young man, to "flee also youthful lusts" — "teen-age lust" as the pop song goes. All young people sin, and sin produces discordant, repellent vibrations which rifle the concert of life until the strings are gutless and flat. The kicks soon lead to kickbacks.

Bad vibrations cause young people to blow their minds. If they use drugs, they get high and then they crash. The Bible speaks of those of a "hostile mind," of those whose "minds were blinded" — leading to a "reprobate mind," to a "doubtful mind," to being "carnally minded," and "shaken in mind" until deeply "troubled in mind," with the result that "a double-minded man is unstable in all his ways."

Drugs are an "in" thing today in affecting the mind. In one northern city, suicides among youth have rocketed up 55 percent in the past year, which is attributed directly to the increased use of drugs. In 1967, the Gallup Poll first asked U.S. college students whether they had ever tried marijuana or LSD. Five percent said they had smoked grass and 1 percent admitted they had dropped acid. By the beginning of 1971 the same poll reported that 42 percent had experimented with marijuana and 14 percent with LSD during the last month. Another poll, dealing with the one million or so young people who take to the roads each summer, revealed that 80 percent had used drugs and 48 percent had used hallucinogens.

The spread of drugs even into such previously wholesome areas as athletics has been indicated in books written by former linebacker Dave Meggysey of pro football's St. Louis Cardinals and former New York Yankee pitcher Jim Bouton.

The American Medical Association cautions that drug abuse is now "a world-wide problem of epidemic proportions." President Nixon has indicated that the use of drugs could affect national security. The nation has been shocked to learn of the high percentage of American troops who have been on drugs in Vietnam.

The tragic effects of heroin, acid dropping, and speed freaking are universally known. National Institute of Mental Health studies have revealed the heavy toll in psychotic episodes that marijuana and hashish seem to induce. In Canada Dr. Fred Lundell released a government report on the effects of marijuana. In seventy pages of evaluation, he revealed the aggravated "paranoid delusions" and other long-term destructiveness which it induced. Summing up, he said, "The fact is, marijuana does produce serious adverse reactions, and to dismiss them by scientific or semantic labeling, or to rationalize that these were psychiatric cases who would go psychotic anyway is a rather cavalier attitude."

Timothy Leary, Harvard professor-turned-prophet of the drug culture, has now been rejected by his bedfellows, the Black Panthers. Speaking from Algiers, Eldridge Cleaver is reported to have become so disenchanted with the "madness" of the psychedelic culture that he placed Timothy Leary in "protective custody." Psychedelic drugs and their accompanying effects, says Cleaver, are "harmful to our cause and counter-revolutionary." Leary himself purportedly concedes this fact and recommends that serious revolutionaries must turn away from turning on with drugs.

In our Knoxville Crusade in 1970, Johnny Cash told the crowd of 62,000 — chiefly young people — who gathered in the University of Tennessee football stadium: "When you take drugs, you may be in ecstasy for a few minutes, but you're soon on the ridge of terror. Take it from a guy who's been there, it ain't worth it." John Lennon, of the Beatles, now says, "I'm against drugs, I really am.... The ideal is to have no drugs." Truly, drugs produce bad vibrations!

A young leader in the California Hell's Angels was usually stoned. Nevertheless, he came to the Crusade at Anaheim Stadium. When the invitation was given, he came forward and made his commitment to Christ. And he became unhooked through a personal experience with Christ.

If you who are hooked, you who have blown your minds on drugs, unreservedly commit yourself to Jesus Christ, you can, as the Bible promises, be "transformed by the renewing of your mind." The Bible promises that "the peace of God shall keep your mind"; that "Thou wilt keep him in perfect peace whose mind is stayed on Thee."

Bad vibrations? Young people feel them in bodies which are being burned out by *bad habits*. You young people have a great deal to say to the older generation about pollution, yet you pollute the air with one of the most harmful of all atmospheric pollutants: cigarette smoke. When I was young the devastating effects of tobacco were not known. Today everyone is aware of its bad vibrations. Jesus said: "Everyone who commits sin is a slave" (John 8:34, NEB). The Apostle Paul talked about "slaves of sin" (Romans 6:20).

Alcoholism is another bad vibration which, in this country, is our third greatest killer. The Bible makes a distinction between temperance and drunkenness. Among young people in America today drinking is for getting drunk. And many go on to become alcoholics. Today we have nearly seven million chronic alcoholics.

Drunkenness is not a new vice. Its ravages have always been a scourge on the human race. However, there is cause for alarm because during the last year drunkenness has begun to increase among students in Europe, North America, and Australia. Alcohol is a killer, a murderer.

Bad vibrations: *sexual sins!* The guilt felt as a result of committing immorality is one of the two chief reasons why so many students on American campuses commit suicide. The two leading sins of ancient Corinth were drunkenness and immorality, and it was with reference to the latter that Paul taught that our humanity was not "made for sexual promiscuity; it was made for God, and God is the answer to our deepest longings" (I Corinthians 6:13, Phillips).

Sexual sins bomb the emotions of youth. A decade ago Marilyn Monroe was the world's sex symbol, and she bombed out through suicide because her life's bad vibrations became unbearable. At the beginning of the seventies perhaps the wildest exponents of sensuality were Jimi Hendrix and Janis Joplin. But it wasn't long before both were dead — at the age of twenty-seven.

Dr. Marion Powell now labels pregnancy as the leading cause of teen-age girls dropping out of school. *The Sensuous Woman* may be a best seller, but it is also a wholesaler of promiscuity, heartbreak, and despair. The book does not tell about the guilt, the broken homes, the sufferings of middle and old age from loneliness and despair. In time, the pleasures of sensuous living turn stale, then destroy.

Not only does immorality often lead to suicide and bring on illegitimacy with its attendant woes, but it also leaves in its wake the dread venereal diseases, gonorrhea and syphilis, which are raging in epidemic proportions.

Among the more tragic results of syphilis are the destruction of brain cells, total blindness and insanity. These consequences can still occur eight or ten years after the original symptoms of the disease have vanished. The American Social Health Association estimates that close to one million people in the United States are walking around with non-infectious syphilis.

The bad vibrations of V.D. can be seen clearly in a letter that one newspaper printed from a girl who signed herself "Scorched and Scared." She said, "This problem is too big for me. My memory is going and my body is full of sores. I need help but who will help me? I can't tell anybody around here what is happening. A while ago, I took a wrong turn and I guess I have VD and the agony and remorse are killing me. Who can help?"

Her unceasing misery is not what *The Sensuous Woman* or *The Sensuous Man* promise. They dramatize only the pleasure, ignoring the despair and the multitude of troubles that follow.

Recently a UCLA student confessed to me that the chief ogre of adolescence is *"guilt."* Guilt is a prominent word among psychoanalysts, psychiatrists, and ministers too. I think I have heard it more often in the last year than ever before.

The dictionary calls guilt "the act or state of having done a wrong or committed an offense." Many psychologists have referred to its "pangs" and its "agonies." Samuel F. Warner says that it is the violation of the law that the Apostle Paul declares is "written within men's hearts which functions to judge one's self." The symptoms of guilt are many but the root cause is one. We have broken the moral law of the universe as expressed in the Ten Commandments and the Sermon on the Mount. So we have a sense of guilt. This guilt causes a variety of psychological problems such as insecurity, tension, hunger for approval, struggles for recognition, etc. A sense of guilt, some psychiatrists point out, is as necessary as a sense of pain. We need both in order to keep us from getting hurt.

The Bible teaches that guilt is inescapable — not just psychological guilt, but guilt toward God. It says that all have broken God's laws and come short of the glory of God. Therefore, guilt rests upon the entire human race. Some persons may feel it more intensely than others, but the guilt is there either in the subconscious or in the conscious. It must be dealt with before we can become normal, fulfilled personalities. This is why Jesus Christ died. He died on the cross to take our guilt away. He shed His blood to "purge our dead conscience from dead works to serve the living and true God." So guilt is not all bad. Without it there is nothing to drive a person toward self-examination and toward God for forgiveness.

At the end of each of my sermons, I give an invitation for people to come forward to receive Christ. It is interesting that I have never had a psychiatrist criticize the invitation — though they may criticize the sermon, the music, or the atmosphere, but never the appeal to find forgiveness. I once asked a psychiatrist friend why this was so. He said, "Because you are giving people a release from their pent-up emotions and sense of guilt." God offers relief and release through the forgiveness that Christ purchased on the cross.

When Jesus was here on earth, He said that for any degree of guilt, "for all manner of sin," that human trespass "shall be forgiven unto man," provided there is repentance and true faith.

In one of our London crusades a young woman who had engaged in prostitution came forward and, having received Christ's forgiveness and fulness of salvation, described her new condition, "I feel so clean inside." Another young woman had left her home in provincial England for London's West End but did not quite make it as an actress. Instead she fell into immorality and dope addiction. Brought to the crusade, she too discovered forgiveness and a brand-new life in Jesus Christ as Lord and Savior. Today she is a missionary in Latin America.

Everywhere, today hearts are empty, and we know that nature abhors a vacuum. If your heart is not attuned to God, it will become a catch basin for every device of the devil. Yes, Satan is at work in our world. The Bible is my authority. He exists and he has control over thousands of young people whose hearts have never been captured by Jesus Christ. He has hundreds of agents writing pornographic literature and producing sex movies to pollute young minds. He has intellectuals in high positions teaching a hedonistic and permissive philosophy. He has recruited even church leaders who are advocating moral promiscuity.

Daily, I come in contact with mixed-up people, young men and women caught in the anguish of their own unpreparedness, intellectuals who have been seduced by false science, and rich men held in the grip of insecurity. They have no commitment to any goal. They lack an anchorage for their real self. And I long to take every one of them by the hand and lead them into the presence of the One who said, "Come unto me, all ye that labor and are heavy laden, and I will give you rest. . . . rest unto your souls."

Augustine was one of the greatest theologians of all time. He was a wild, intemperate, immoral youth. In spite of his mother's pleadings and prayers, he grew worse instead of better. But one day he had a personal encounter with Jesus Christ that transformed his life. His restlessness and the practice of sin disappeared. He became one of the great saints of all time.

John Newton was a slave trader on the west coast of Africa. One day in a storm at sea he met Jesus Christ. He went back to England and became an Anglican clergyman. He wrote scores of fine hymns, one of which has become the modern popular song, "Amazing Grace."

This is what Christ can do for anyone who puts his trust in Him.

5

THE SEX HANG-UP

Most young people today have some sort of sex hang-up. This has been true in every generation. But today it is probably more acute than at any other time in history. But I doubt if you know the extent to which you are coerced, maneuvered, tempted, exploited and bedeviled by commercial interests who support sex for their economic advantage. Wherever you turn, sex rears its head. Always the impression is left that the practice of fornication and adultery is commonplace and acceptable. Few speak out against immorality or present the real hazards of promiscuity. Surrounded by this type of mentality and environment, you young people must make a decision about your own sexual behavior.

And it's a lonely decision — who likes to make decisions anyway? "What's the hurry? I'll worry about that when I come to it."

But until you make that decision, you are playing with fire. In the meantime, you are making dozens of small and ostensibly insignificant decisions about sex. You are experiencing glances, touches, thoughts, and you are embracing or resisting them.

This is how it works: You see an attractive person of the opposite sex, and you wonder if . . . you wonder if. . . .

"So, what's wrong with that?"

Unknowingly, you are preparing yourself for seduction.

Your lines are memorized. In your mind you have already gone all the way.

I ask you to make a choice now!

I ask you to commit yourself to sex within marriage and only within marriage.

You might ask: Why do so many young people do it? Why some of my best friends? The leaders of my class? People I most admire?

Let's examine some of the factors.

We have a *sex-saturated culture* of which our news media is a part. It is supposed to present the news truthfully and accurately. But what happens? People want sensationalism and will pay for it. Unfortunately, many editors, writers, producers and directors give it to them. Along with national news, they publish scandals, one following another, until readers accept immorality as a normal way of life.

Then there are the *cultural anthropologists*. Occasionally they come up with an alleged "discovery" bearing on morality and decency. If they dissent from tradition, that becomes news. I recall hearing of an anthropologist who claimed to have investigated 350 or so cultures and "discovered" that seven out of ten permitted sexual experimentation prior to marriage. Newspapers reported the story plus his advocacy that churches recognize the situation and sponsor permissive experimentation. Radio and television broadcast his statement, implying that most of the world's communities indulged in premarital sex and that talk about retribution or sin was outdated. Many young people believed him because his thesis supported their natural desires.

But how could one man investigate 350 societies when it takes a lifetime to study even one? How could any researcher know or even guess whether or not premarital sex left psychological scars among all those ancient clans, tribes, and nations? In fact, he could not. Nevertheless, our youth quickly added his "findings" to the mythology of permissive sex. Today this mythology has become all-powerful. Every time I undertake a dialogue with young people, I must deal with it. Even if that professor had been truthful and his findings accurate, it would not prove that sexual experimentation was right any more than if he discovered that 350 tribes had practiced the murder of unwanted babies.

Another influence on sexual behavior is *peer pressure*. The dictionary says that one's peer is another person of the same general rank, age, ability; in short, an equal. My son's peers, for instance, are his friends, classmates, and teammates. When a number of them (or their leaders) begin to think in a certain way and when they begin to "put down" all those who think otherwise, they are exerting peer pressure. In essence they say, "Conform or get lost." Since no one enjoys losing friends or being cast out of his own circle, peer pressure — especially during the years of adolescence — is an almost irresistible force.

Researchers have found that peer pressure exerted within a clique has caused every one of its members to experiment with drugs, to engage in murderous gang fights, to steal autos, and to violate the seventh commandment. Peer pressure accounts for much of the promiscuous sex in high schools and colleges.

A colleague told me of receiving a letter from a student who wrote: "I get home only every two or three months but when I do, my girl friend (we're engaged) insists that I have relations with her. She says her sorority requires it. I'm no prude and I hope to be married someday, but I feel that this sex bit is unhealthy for our relationship."

Some young people have other reasons. Given the environment of an unhappy home life or an unsatisfied hunger for love or popularity, a girl may decide that anything is better than the emotional limbo in which she lives. If she surrenders her virtue, it is usually because she has a reason, not a valid one, but reasonable enough to justify her action to herself.

All young people yearn for recognition as individuals. They say, "I want to be myself!" What many of them mean is that they don't want anyone telling them what they must do. We all know the saying, "She got married to get away from home." She might be reacting to neglect, overdiscipline, or overprotection. Regardless, she was ready to listen to one who gave her the feeling that she counted as a person. Dr. Evelyn Duvall thumbnails the situation thus: "The young person (girl or boy) who feels unloved, misunderstood, rejected, and neglected is far more likely to indulge in premarital intercourse than is the one who knows real and continuing love." [1]

Young men have a different problem. Whereas girls mature about two years earlier than boys and require a longer time for arousal, male arousal is easy and almost instantaneous. In their late teens young men are at the peak of their sexual powers and are bursting with hormones. They want to make the right decisions, but Lydia G. Dawes of Boston's Children's Hospital says this is difficult. "How can anyone think clearly during a bombardment? He (the boy) is being shaken within by his urges." [2]

The source of stimulation can be a movie, magazine, lewd joke, or a smile from a passing girl. What follows is like a chain reaction. Reason deserts you. Satisfaction and release become all-important. As a rule you believe that your date feels exactly as you feel and is equally eager and impatient. You don't even suspect that, in the majority of cases, you are wrong. You have told me, "Girls lead me on!" Yes, but usually because they want to please you. With rare exceptions, they are much happier when they are not cajoled or pressured into "going all the way."

"The girl plays at sex, for which she is not ready, because what she wants fundamentally is love; and the boy plays at love, for which he is not ready, because what he wants is sex," says Dr. Mary Calderone. "We must understand that in reality both boy and girl seek love and sex, tenderness and passion, but that in the early years their drives are rarely synchronized."[3]

Playing at love is the great American, undergraduate pastime, and it is booby-trapped for both sexes. Action is much easier than thought, yet I know that you young people do think and reach conclusions and wonder if you are right. You write me questions by the thousands, and I answer all that I can through my newspaper column and on radio and television. Your concern is always healthy but your ignorance is often abysmal. In substance, here are some of the questions I get most often.

QUESTION: We are in the midst of a sex revolution. Why don't you admit it?

ANSWER: I would say we are going through a sexual tempest, a bombardment provided by the unprecedented exploitation of cheap sex by moviemakers, theater owners, publishers, and producers of pornography. But our sex habits have not changed nearly as much as the openness of talk about sex. You are more open about everything. You accept public nudity. You are beginning to accept homosexuality. But youthful participation in premarital sex, as stated earlier, has increased only a little. This is the verdict of many qualified observers. Answering your question, I must reply, "Sex revolution, no! But sex pollution? Yes!!!"

QUESTION: But everybody is doing it!

ANSWER: Everybody? Among my notes taken from the findings of many researchers, I find these statistics:

"National figures indicate that about twenty-five percent of high school students have sex relations before marriage. Many others come very close to it but do not complete the sex act." Thus everybody is not doing it. If you are doing it, you may be in the minority! That may surprise some of you, but statistics confirm it. So my answer is that *everybody* is *not* doing it. Don't allow bull-session boasting by "with it" cliques to confuse your thinking.

QUESTION: What I do in my sex life is my private business. Why should parents or anyone else have a right to criticize me?

ANSWER: Young people are strong on privacy. What they often overlook is the consequence of their "private" act. I know of a minister who tells his young people about a father who had the problem of making his son understand the hazards of immorality. Finally he gave the lad a hammer and some nails. After each offense (lying, cheating, etc.) the boy had to drive a nail into the door of his room. When he apologized, the nail could be pulled out. Very soon, the youth noted that even though he withdrew the nail immediately, the hole remained. "And that is what happens to your character," the minister declared. "You can try to right every wrong, but each offense leaves a scar."

QUESTION: Doesn't premarital sex help an engaged couple learn whether or not they are compatible sexually?

ANSWER: This is a myth. Doctors tell me that the male and the female bodies are designed so sympathetically that practically every mating is mechanically satisfactory. "Instances of serious and permanent difficulty are rare," one physician writes. "In other words, as a test of suitability, premarital intercourse tells us nothing of significance that cannot be discovered in other ways," such as a physical examination. So the truth is just the opposite and statistics prove that marriages are much more lasting when the couple has *never* practiced premarital sex. It may take weeks or months to adjust to one another. A clandestine affair might well lead the young people to think they are physically unsuited, whereas if they waited for sex within marriage, such problems could be worked out.

QUESTION: Is it not true that once a person is aroused it is unhealthy to "turn him off" without satisfying him? If a man is restrained, isn't this bad for him? Don't normal people need sex?

ANSWER: Helen Jean Burn talks of "turning him off" in *Better Than the Birds, Smarter Than the Bees.* "It's no joke.

It aches!" she says. "When the boy becomes sexually aroused, hormones are secreted which cause the vein taking blood out to close off." [4] However, there is no known harm, she advises.

Some young men seem to think that if they don't get satisfaction they may go crazy. This myth is so widely held that the U.S. Army took notice of it. Army chaplains were given a message to pass on to every soldier. Signed by 300 doctors, it said: "We, the undersigned members of the medical profession, testify to our belief that continence has not been shown to be detrimental to health or virility; that there is no evidence of its being inconsistent with the highest physical, mental and moral efficiency."

Self-restraint means some discomfort and much self-discipline. During adolescence, every fiber in your being will be under stress. This is a time of awakening, of the birth of an adult. It is like being thirsty but not allowed to drink, or of being hungry and not allowed to eat, with the difference that your body cannot survive without water and food. But you can survive without sex — actually your body can become stronger. If your sexual power is sublimated — that's a psychologist's word for transferring your sex energy to another form of expression — it can produce great mental, physical and psychological benefits.

Your sex powers before marriage might be likened to the savings a young man puts in the bank to purchase a home when he weds. Your powers are not squandered nor is your moral future mortgaged. Your powers are *sublimated* — put in the bank — for future use.

QUESTION: If God made us what we are and the desire for sex is natural, why should we not do whatever comes naturally?

ANSWER: God made you and provided sex for your use, but He expects you to observe the rules, laws and suggestions He laid down plus the common sense with which He endowed you. Rightly used, sex is a blessing. But abused, it can turn into a curse. Sex is a wonderful servant but a terrible master.

QUESTION: If we love each other and intend to get married, and if we are not hurting anyone, why should we wait?

ANSWER: Three big "if's" are involved: If you love each other, if you get married, and if you don't hurt anyone. Let's take them one at a time.

If you love. . . . Helen Jean Burn points out that "adolescents love deeply, for three or four months — not always but many times! So a sexual relationship comes along and this requires a commitment, not just for a three-four month period. It is supposed to last. But it doesn't, and then what? When things go wrong, then you are back where you started, and maybe worse off. The boy has a scalp for his "group," but he has a lot of guilt feelings too. And the girl is more insecure than ever, just because a relationship she believed in didn't last." [5]

Or maybe your understanding of love is incomplete. In *Sin, Sex, and Self-Control* Dr. Norman Vincent Peale describes a conversation with a boy who claimed he was in love. The youth said, "I've found the right girl. . . . I knew what I wanted her to be like — pretty, intelligent, and a lot of personality."

Dr. Peale asked: "Isn't that a rather narrow, even selfish approach to love? You are really saying, 'This is what *I* want. This is what *I* must have.' Apparently you're more concerned with what you can get out of this relationship than what you can give. Is that right?"

The youth denied his selfishness so Dr. Peale asked: "Do you care about her welfare? About her peace of mind? About her long-range happiness?"

"Of course I do!"

The young man really thought he did, but here is what Dr. Peale had to tell him: "In that case, I don't see how you can justify asking her or persuading her to sleep with you before you are married. You are putting her in jeopardy, in danger, in a situation where at the very least she'll have to struggle with her conscience . . . disregard the ideals her parents have tried to implant in her, perhaps violate the moral teachings of her religion. Is this an act of love? It seems to me it's just the reverse. Real love, if you want a rough definition, is the willingness to put someone else's welfare and happiness ahead of your own desires. That's precisely what you are *not* doing. So maybe you're *not* in love." [6]

Waldo Beach calls real love, *real* love, "the settled disposition to seek the well-being of 'the other' as precious and sacred." We see it often in a mother's love for her child, less often between married persons. Don't confuse it with sex. Abigail Van Buren advises: "Sex says 'Anyone will do.' Love says, 'No one else will do, just that certain someone.' Love can't be stolen, transferred, bought or sold. It must be given."

A young man wrote me: "I think of nothing else but her. I know I am in love, and I want to enjoy her body as well as her mind. Why should I wait?"

Look into your mirror, young man, and answer your own question. Tell yourself that you are asking her for sex for *her* good. Tell yourself that you are submerging all of your wishes in favor of hers. And listen to your conscience.

If you get married. . . . Plans do go awry so consider this possibility, as Dr. Peale did when he talked to the same young man mentioned earlier. "Suppose you fall out of love," he suggested. "Do you think your girl will be just as attractive and desirable to somebody else after her love affair with you? Or will she be a little secondhand? . . . Put yourself in the place of the man who may eventually marry this girl of yours. Wouldn't you resent the faceless person — or persons — who preceded you? Look back at that neat little check list of yours and see if one of your requirements isn't a girl who is pure. Am I right?"

The youth said, "You're right, but we'll be married soon and then everything will be all right."

But would they? Dr. Peale reminded him of his admission that he wanted a girl with high moral standards. But now he expected her to relax those standards for him. If she does, surrendering her virginity, what of their married tranquillity? "Long after you are married," Dr. Peale concluded, "those elastic standards may come back to haunt you. You may even find yourself wondering if you can really trust your wife." [7] It has happened. It will happen again.

If you don't hurt anybody. . . . "Who is to get hurt?" Look at yourself, at your family, your friends and society. For what other reason than being "hurt" have civilized people been so concerned about premarital relations for so many centuries? Greek and Roman families worried about it, as did our American ancestors. Back in 1871, a public debate was held at Harvard University on the question: "Whether it is fornication to lay with one's sweetheart before marriage?"

It takes no poll for those of us who have communicated with young people to know the devastation that permissive sexual activity generally causes. It becomes a cancer in the bodies and minds and characters of those who indulge, almost without exception. And there are other victims, such innocent bystanders as parents, grandparents, old family friends, teachers, and advisors, all much more concerned than you can understand. They want only the best for you. Anything less than a happy marital voyage gives them pain. The wisdom of their years says that premarital relations are always a mistake.

I have heard you argue that: "I am not concerned about others, nor about society." But you are society. If you engage in premarital relations you are living with an attitude which produces 300,000 illegitimate babies every year. "And that affects society," says Dr. Peale. And so do "heaven knows how many abortions, forced marriages, consequent divorces — all that puts quite a dent in society." [8]

Who else gets hurt? What of the illegitimate baby? What of him and his rights? Surely he deserves a home and loving, responsible parents! Are you ready to provide such things? So the baby is put up for adoption and the agency puts him in a loving, responsible home. Do you think for one second the real mother can ever forget her child? She is scarred and haunted for life. I know of one such baby, now grown, who says, "I'll always wonder where my mother is and if she needs me."

What about V.D.? In countries where sexual permissiveness has become acceptable, V.D. has reached epidemic proportions, even with every modern scientific device known to man. And for some there is *no* known cure.

If you love, *if* you marry, *if* you hurt no one — those "if's" can haunt you. Go back to your mirror, young man. Go back to your mirror, young lady. To be blunt, to be honest, to be at all helpful, I must say to you, "You've got to be kidding if you think such things cannot happen!"

But they do, and one of the reasons is passion. Dr. Marion Hilliard describes the monster: "It is a savage power that can leap out of control without the slightest warning. Passion is relentless, rushing into any vacuum, driving on to its own satisfaction regardless of the havoc that may follow. Passion has no morals, no standards, no control, no compassion. It is cruel and devouring, seeking immediate fulfillment. Passion tosses aside rules, ethics, civilization, individual plans and intentions. It disregards dignity and grace, is humorless and full of rage." [9]

Now I want you to turn to the Bible for God's answer concerning this philosophical, psychological and spiritual gift called sex. Until now my discussion has been based on practicality and good common sense. Now turn with me to the Scriptures, to God's message and wisdom which is as relevant today as the day it was written — because it is eternal!

The Bible teaches that God created sex. He made "male and female." Then it says, "God saw every thing that he had made, and, behold, it was very good." This included the natural, sexual attraction between the man and the woman He had created. Therefore, sex is not sin! It is God's gift to the human race. It is for procreation; for enjoyment within the bonds of matrimony; for the fulfillment of married love.

Soon after the creation, because of Adam's and Eve's rebellion and the introduction of sin into the human race, God had to add some guidelines. One is the seventh commandment which says: "Thou shalt not commit adultery." Adultery is when a married person engages in sex outside of his marriage bond. Fornication involves sex between unmarried people. The Bible has dire warnings concerning both.

Bill Gothard has listed the various words used in the New Testament that deal with this sin. It is quite evident that God not only judges the action but the thoughts and intents of the heart also (see Matthew 5:28).

Lasciviousness: This word means "the tendency to excite lustful desires." ". . . deceit, lasciviousness, an evil eye, blasphemy, pride, foolishness: all these evil things come from within, and defile the man" (Mark 7:22-23). "I shall bewail many which have sinned already, and have not repented of the uncleanness and fornication and lasciviousness which they have committed" (2 Corinthians 12:21). "Now the works of the flesh are manifest, which are these: adultery, fornication, uncleanness, lasciviousness" (Galatians 5:19). "Who being past feeling have given themselves over unto lasciviousness" (Ephesians 4:19). "For there are certain men crept in unawares . . . ungodly men, turning the grace of our God into lasciviousness, and denying the only Lord God, and our Lord Jesus Christ" (Jude 4).

Sensuality: This is the planned appeal to the physical senses for personal gratification. It is the preoccupation with bodily or sexual pleasure, whether through reading a pornographic book, watching a sex movie, or engaging in heavy petting. "This wisdom descendeth not from above, but is earthly, sensual, devilish" (James 3:15). "These be they who separate themselves, sensual, having not the Spirit" (Jude 19).

Concupiscence: This word carries with it the idea of a strong or abnormal sexual desire or appetite. In the days of Noah the people were given over to "evil imaginations." It seemed that all they could think about was lust and sex. This is one of the reasons why God judged them. "But sin, taking occasion by the commandment, wrought in me all manner of concupiscence" (Romans 7:8). "Mortify therefore your members which are upon the earth; fornication, uncleanness, inordinate affection, evil concupiscence" (Colossians 3:5). "For this is the will of God, even your sanctification . . . not in the lust of concupiscence" (1 Thessalonians 4:3, 5).

Reprobation: Reprobates are the totally depraved people. Their conscience is either dead or seared. They can no longer blush. They have lost the ability to discern between good and evil. Many of the people who write pornographic literature reach this terrifying position. "And even as they did not like to retain God in their knowledge, God gave them over to a reprobate mind, to do those things which are not convenient" (Romans 1:28). "These also resist the truth: men of corrupt minds, reprobate concerning the faith" (2 Timothy 3:8). "They profess that they know God; but in works they deny him, being abominable, and disobedient, and unto every good work reprobate" (Titus 1:16).

Fornication: As we have already noted, this is the voluntary sexual intercourse between an unmarried man and woman. This is premarital sex relations. Note what the Scriptures say: "Now the body is not for fornication, but for the Lord, and the Lord for the body" (1 Corinthians 6:13). "Flee fornication . . . he that committeth fornication sinneth against his own body" (1 Corinthians 6:18). "For this is the will of God, even your sanctification, that ye should abstain from fornication" (1 Thessalonians 4:3). "Know ye not that the unrighteous shall not inherit the kingdom of God? Be not deceived: fornicators . . . (shall not) inherit the kingdom of God" (1 Corinthians 6:9). "Looking diligently lest any man fail of the grace of God . . . Lest there be any fornicator, or profane person" (Hebrews 12:15, 16).

Perhaps it should be noted that chastity is a peculiarly Christian virtue. William Barclay brings this out in his New Testament commentary. In the ancient world immorality was the *norm*.

Enough of such examples! You can see that the Bible definitely teaches that immorality is a sin in the sight of God. It hurts you psychologically and physically — and it hurts other people.

The Bible advocates self-control. Young unmarried men are instructed in Proverbs to refrain from promiscuity with loose women. Paul urges young Timothy to "keep thyself pure" and to "control your turbulent and impulsive sexual desires." Again, he says: "It is God's will that you should keep pure in person, that you should practice abstinence from sexual immorality."

Sex outside of marriage is sin! But "sin" is a word we rarely hear these days. In an article in *Good Housekeeping* magazine, Phyllis McGinley reinforces my faith in the old-fashioned gumption of American mothers. Writing of her daughters, she says that they knew how babies were born and they had been gently instructed in sex. But she worried that their sexuality might become a flood and she sought a message for them that would be a positive help. "It's an iconoclastic thing," she decided, "but I shall remind my daughters simply that there is such a thing as right and wrong. I shall commit the dreadful heresy of talking about sin. . . . My daughters shall be told that there exists a moral law and an ancient Commandment; and that they do wrong who flout them."

And if there is an exceptionally stubborn problem with her children, she will solve it by using another old-time device. She first learned of its power from her oldest daughter. They had been arguing about some action that could not be tolerated when the child burst out with, "Oh, mother, why don't you just tell me *not to* for once, and stop explaining!"

From the beginning of time, children have respected the power of a positive "No." They may put up all kinds of arguments. They may even disobey. But they respect a parent's disapproval of what they know deep in their heart to be wrong.

The Bible teaches: "Flee youthful lusts" (2 Timothy 2:22). Any type of sexual arousal encourages youthful lusts. If you drive a car without a license, you are asking for trouble. If you stimulate your lust periodically without a license, one day you will get into trouble.

Many young people ask the question: How can we distinguish the sexual desire that is a gift from God from lust?

Someone has said that the first look is not a sin — it is the second look. A boy may admire a beautiful girl. There is nothing wrong in that. It is when he begins to undress her in his mind and to allow his thoughts to engage in sexual fantasies that it becomes lust.

But what about love? How can you be certain? I suggest these simple measures that you can apply to yourself. Is your love patient? Is it considerate? Can it wait until marriage for physical fulfillment? Paul wrote that true love "suffereth long." Experience says that true love's patience is inexhaustible. True love does not assert itself, claim rights or demand privileges. It always thinks first of the other person. The Biblical phrase is it "vaunteth not itself." True love never thinks evil of the beloved. It is never suspicious but always supportive and inspiring. True love bears all things. Nothing weakens or undermines it. It is a rock, an anchorage, a foundation for all the years to come.

These simple tests are a mirror that millions have used. Physiologists, psychiatrists, and marriage counselors attest to their validity. They were first recommended almost two thousand years ago by a man named Paul in First Corinthians 13. That chapter provides the finest definition of love the world has received.

In concluding this chapter I suggest these measures for getting the sexual drive under control: To begin with, remember that sex isn't *everything*. Exciting and mysterious, yes, but it is only one facet of our wonderful world of experiences. Don't allow it to dominate your life.

Keep it in perspective! Be grateful that God has given you creative powers, but be careful about your use and your abuse of them, and follow *His* rules.

Face the facts honestly and realistically. Recognize that premarital or extramarital sex brings misery and tragedy into your life and the lives of others. But most of all face the fact that sex outside of marriage is a sin against God.

Let the Master, Jesus Christ, assume control of this aspect of your life. Surveys show that Christian young people (though even they have a full supply of problems) are not so easily tripped up as are those who are not anchored to a faith in Christ. The Bible tells us that Christ "was in all points tempted like as we are, yet without sin" (Hebrews 4: 15). He wrestled with the same problems. Yet He triumphed! His desires were under control! And He will stand with you in your hour of temptation. With the Holy Spirit in your heart providing spiritual power, your desires may also be controlled — and transformed to a more noble purpose.

If you have not won your battle of sex, you have not won the battle of life. I earnestly believe that God has made a promise that He will fulfill if you allow it. "Except the Lord build the house, they labor in vain who build it," said the psalmist. Take God into your sex life, your courtship, and your marriage and then your home can become a heaven on earth.

I was in my teens when I accepted Christ as the Master of my life. And I have found the Scripture to be true when it says: "He always causeth us to triumph!" We cannot avoid all troubles or temptations. But we do have His promise: "In all these things, we are more than conquerors." God *can* help you with your sex hang-up.

6
COPPING OUT

More than a decade ago the American president focused national attention on young Americans by inviting them to help change their world by enlisting in the U. S. Peace Corps. Not since the euphoric days of Teddy Roosevelt had young people flashed to the fore with such flair and attractiveness. But presently, observers of the American scene made a grim discovery. As President Kennedy soon declared. "We are in danger of losing our will to fight, to sacrifice, to endure. The slow corrosion of luxury is already beginning to show."

We were also in danger of losing much more, as we soon learned. Young Americans whose forebears had set their faces toward a plunging frontier, who had survived a civil war, who had fought two world wars to stave off the tyranny of totalitarianism, who had toiled through the drought and hunger of a terrible depression, these youthful Americans, in the eyes of our late president, were showing signs of dropping out.

His warning was a prelude to an astonishing change. Soon, the idols of youth would be anti-heroes with long hair and beards, displacing brush-cut, all-American types. Soon, the gleaming hot rods of the Flourishing Fifties would be passé as status symbols. Instead, the average youth would become a pedestrian or a hitch-hiker, roaming the open road. He would reject punching time clocks, meeting timetables, and taking showers. He, his brothers, and his sisters would migrate into the parks, the meadows, or the mountains, leaving clock and calendar with a program-minded generation. Becoming a military hero by risking his life to fight for home and country would lose its appeal. A growing minority would gather with disheveled contemporaries to seek their place in the sun by smoking pot. They might even burn the flag. Rather than conform to the American ideal of being dynamic and vibrant with enterprise, he would prefer to do his own thing, submerge his future in a subculture, and fly in the face of traditional idealism. Academicians, athletes, technocrats, and politicians no longer would be enshrined as heroes.

Why strain to be a beauty queen, to become a Miss America? Why endure an unending schedule of nerve-wracking appearances when you could hold up two fingers for peace, ignore the cosmetic counter, and sit down with your flower-power friends and take a drug trip to Paradise? By the middle-sixties, American vigor had come to a stop. The young horses were balking; they were kicking over the traces; worse, they had jumped over the race track fence just as their elders had expected them to come thundering down the homestretch. Suddenly, they were nibbling the grass in the infield.

By the late sixties and early seventies, dropping out had replaced digging in. The "cop-out" had become the human symbol of being "with it" and "where the action is." Though most young Americans continued to pursue the traditional goals of academic excellence, athletic victories, and unimpeachable character, a noisy minority applauded the new hero. Slick magazines spread his picture and his gospel. The freak was good copy and he attracted imitators. Al Capp says he created his prototype originally for his comic strip "Li'l Abner," never dreaming he would actually come to life.

So the cop-out — what *my p*eers called "goofing off" — became a fact of life. Presently, a movie title declared, "Stop the World! I Want to Get Off!" And thousands agreed. But copping out offers no real remedy for the cosmic ailments that sicken our cities and soften our citizens. Cringing before a murderer has never stopped a killing. And our hard-won freedoms of thought, imagination, and expression are being murdered.

What we — your generation and mine — must do now is to discover who we really are, where we are, and how we got here. You need to understand why your generation is so extraordinary and different from all that have gone before, and why you, despite your quirks and confusion, are such a special person. You cannot change the world until those questions are answered. So let us explore a bit of history, a bit of philosophy, and a bit of theology in pursuit of the truth that can make us whole.

The phenomenon of copping out probably began in homes where ambitious parents had pushed their offspring a little too hard. It was undoubtedly advanced by confrontations with teachers and by hassles with officials. When young people observed what the original drop-outs were doing in the Haight-Ashbury and North Beach sections of San Francisco, in New York's East Village, and in London's King Street, their reckless way of life seemed to offer an escape. As the pressure built up, they began to sniff glue and to listen endlessly to hard rock and the new country music.

Joining others of the same persuasion, girls and boys alike, they followed the example of their new heroes and moved to a thousand hippie pads. Newspapers and commentators called it the youth subculture. Sociologists wrote books about it. And parents, tuned out by deafening music and freak friends, began to go quietly mad.

At first, for the young converts, it was great. The tall grass was a place to hide, a place to get high and dream with fellow-freaks of an unseen, fantastic world. This was the spaced-out way to be in clover. "Strawberry" fields competed with football fields for the weekender. To swing was the thing. It got one away from the square scene.

With William Hedgepeth, a chronicler of the hippie movement, many youths felt that they were: "trapped within vast cathedrals of thought, simmering, hungering for physical contact yet spinning out our mental energies in empty arabesques. It's time to go, to run, to rise up, fling up the window, thaw the blood, prance high in the wet grass, to shout and feel and seek new rootholds in the nourishing earth. Rise up now beyond your head. Peel the plastic from your eyeballs and revel at long last in a new rapport with earth and air and your own unfettered impulses." [1]

For years, I had told young people that the only way they could change the world was by first changing themselves. And now, by the hundreds of thousands, they were changing before our eyes. But would this kind of change heal their own and society's sores. Most of us doubted it. Many of us did not like what we saw.

The hippie instinct has deep roots. Once, they were called gypsies. In my boyhood, we called them hobos. They strummed banjos and sang yodeling songs. They refused to work; they bummed rides on freight trains, hitchhiked, and drifted. They were not professional thieves, but they were weary of social pressures, and so they lived by ripping off, like some hippies today.

My friend Sam Cole, before he became a follower of Jesus, had been "King of the Hobos" for a generation. Sam had traveled to all but seventeen of the world's countries. He said working was for horses, and he preached goodwill and brotherhood. He took odd jobs, but mostly he sponged. Everywhere he went, he said, he met droves of people who were fed up on working just to pay off the loan companies. His advice? Drop out! But most of the hobos vanished in the early forties.

A more direct ancestor was the beatnik. He was an intellectual, a poet, an artist, and a dissident. San Francisco was his original home. When the mass media discovered him in the fifties, he blossomed into a tourist attraction and then a movement, with Allen Ginsberg, David Meltzer and Lawrence Ferlinghetti as poets laureate. When novelist Jack Kerouac wrote *The Dharma Bums,* the rush was on. By the thousands, young people adopted his Zen slogans, calling it "hip" talk.

Kerouac's other novel, *On the Road*, introduced a James Dean-ish type of hero, uncommitted, rebellious, and a maverick. All the nonconformist train needed was a track. The beatniks built that track. They claimed they were trying to make sense of a crazy world and that their satirical dress and conduct would demonstrate that ultimate harmony would come only to those whose insanity matched that of society. They rapped a lot about reality. Norman F. Cantor in his *Age of Protest* says: "As the beats saw it, reality left no room for the worship of reason. Evil could not be legislated out of society. Nature, history and humanity could not be controlled. Progress, the victim of every war, was an illusion. Death was the central reality." [2] Their philosophy was that of Albert Camus and Jean Paul Sartre. Their style was initially a combination of the mumblings of an absent-minded professor, the posturing of the zoot suiter of the late thirties, and the buffoonery of a Ringling Brothers' clown. They were received with mingled anger and amusement.

Like other seers, philosophers and religious prophets, these speckled birds diagnosed the human condition with uncanny precision. Evil is in the nature of things and cannot be removed by legislation. Man and all that he touches is corrupt and he eventually loses control. This analysis was exactly on target from the Christian point of view, and more accurate than much twentieth century theology which looked at human nature through rose-colored glasses.

Their crucial error was their prescription for curing human ills. In essence, their credo read: (a) Progress is a false doctrine, (b) Imminent death (perhaps the ever present bomb) makes planning folly, (c) Live for today alone, live until the senses sing; do it here and now. It was essentially the same philosophy expressed by Hugh Hefner with his Bunny girls and *Playboy* magazine. But Hefner went first-class and soon made his glossy magazine one of the most popular in the world. The beatniks preferred simplicity and a primitive life style.

If only they had begun their program with God! The first and second commandments are the only therapy the world has ever needed. "Thou shalt love the Lord thy God with all thy heart, and with all thy soul, and with all thy mind. . . . Thou shalt love thy neighbor as thyself."

Those beatniks "begat" both the hippies and the New Left. The beats had deliberately separated themselves from other students by wearing beards and stained levis, and they indulged in kicks they could realize through their eyes, ears and skin. Otherwise they kept their cool.

Their successors, the hippies, added long hair, beads, necklaces, headbands, bells and flowers, and were soon nicknamed "flower children." Neither parents nor police officials were amused when they learned that the latter also treated their bodies as electro-chemical power plants, going from marijuana to hash, to speed, to LSD, and eventually to mainlining on heroin. Their first nationally known centers were the Haight-Ashbury section of San Francisco and the East Village in New York, but a network of unofficial franchises quickly burgeoned from coast to coast. And presently, from continent to continent.

So thousands dropped out. They lived from hand to mouth, on money from home, and on earnings from occasional jobs, panhandling and freeloading. They formed communes or pads of ten to thirty people, each chipping in his bit and in turn hoping for a bite. They surreptitiously passed dope and drugs to each other with or without cost. They communicated through their bodies. "Please touch" became a way of life.

In 1967, they hit the headlines with their first "human be-in." The scene was San Francisco's Golden Gate Park. Press and TV sent battalions of photographers who spread the story. At first, they displayed a certain winsomeness. They were young, sincere, and inordinately pleased to be doing their own thing. The irony was that each person's "own thing" was just like all the others. Most important, they were free. By mid-summer, additional thousands were flooding the nation's "Hashburys," among them runaways, drop-outs, curiosity seekers, students, psychopaths, and drug-pushers moving in for the kill.

Norman F. Cantor's *Age of Protest* describes the consequent bedlam. Idealism competed with tragedy. A hippie group called the Diggers, named after a seventeenth century band of Utopianists, collected clothing and food for new arrivals, giving it away free. "But the summer proved to be a bad scene, a bad trip, despite Diggers' efforts, despite the Hip Job Corps . . . despite the Free Medical Clinic, and despite all the love and flowers. The summer hippie had nowhere to live. . . . They slept in the streets and the doorways. They begged from tourists, took impure LSD, got hooked on methedrine." [3]

Things became so bad in this San Francisco utopia that the Hashbury gurus decided to wind things up with a funeral. Filling a coffin with beads, bells, clarinets, kazoos, guitars, Zen manuals, and water pipes, they hoisted it to their shoulders and paraded through Hashbury for the last time, proclaiming a Brotherhood of Free Men and tossing the coffin symbolically on a flaming funeral pyre. Next day the groovy shops and crash pads began to close.

But the cop-out religion had spread like a contagion. Young people gathered in huge sit-ins, lie-ins, teach-ins, and love-ins. I remember being in Winnipeg, Canada, when a crowd of 3,000 youths had gathered on the lawn in front of the Provincial Parliament buildings. After one of the crusade meetings I put on a cap, a sweat shirt, and dark glasses and attended their love-in. I watched these young people doing their thing. With some of it I was disgusted, but I was overcome with compassion. They were like sheep without a shepherd. Involved in an orgy of quest for meaning in their lives, they seemed to be searching for someone who could give them authoritative answers. The next Sunday hundreds of these young people came to our meeting and scores came forward to find their answer in the Person of Jesus Christ.

Their movement peaked in the summer of 1969 at Woodstock, New York, when almost a half million youths gathered to listen to rock bands, smoke pot, rap with each other, and to say symbolically that the needs of human beings were more important than winning in Vietnam or going to the moon.

Though rock festivals now seem to be out, the appeal of hippiedom continues. Once fiercely anti-Establishment, the movement now has its own establishment which some have called the Disestablishment. It is firmly based on hundreds of campuses, parks, and village squares around the world. Its heroes are the singers of the music their poets have composed. Its uniform is long hair, midnight-cowboy jackets, leather fringes, Indian beads, and bell-bottoms.

A primitive life style has often been an attractive option for people who have found the world too brutal and too complex to endure. Its emulators include many Hindu mystics, certain ancient and medieval monastic orders, several Buddhist sects. In the more inglorious column, for those whose wicks have burned low, it may be the least intolerable option open to them.

But what of the young people themselves? Has their renunciation and rejection of the square way of life healed society? Has it healed their own malaise? Obviously, not. So if we are truly concerned, no matter what our generation, we must understand the causes underlying their retreat, and then we must make a judgment.

We can begin with the *impact on youth of the mass media.* Marshall McLuhan has written that TV produced a global village within whose limits we all now live. Its citizens, he says, react to electronic and print stimuli in identical emotional patterns. Today, panic is piled on panic as we listen, watch, and read. As an experiment, he suggests that you count the impacts per day on your eyes, ears, and brain, flung into your mind-stream with all the shock-power that clever communicators can muster. Alexander Klein calls it "media overkill." And he observes dourly, "The republic is bleeding to death and we stand by watching as though it were a spectator sport." [4] So many youth feel trapped, and they decide that their only option is dropping out.

What has trapped them? Another factor, which is fairly recent, is their *extended adolescence*. Did you know that in earlier periods of history adolescence was virtually unknown? As soon as one married, one became an adult. Marriages took place at age fourteen to sixteen. Today, sheepskins and diplomas must be acquired ahead of a wife. Today, the span between childhood and adulthood may extend over ten years.

Deferred adulthood is synonymous with deferred responsibility. Also required is the postponement of such aspects of maturity as making decisions about life and commitments that are necessary to a "fulfilled life." Most important, it forces the student into an unnaturally passive role at a time when every instinct cries out for participation in the challenges of his twenties.

We adults are much concerned today about trusting our young people. Some of us fear their lack of experience. It is interesting to me that a twenty-year-old Greek or Roman youth was sometimes an officer commanding an army or a soldier conquering an empire for his emperor or king. Alexander the Great was only twenty-one when he conquered the Balkans, twenty-two when he crossed the Hellespont, and twenty-four when he established the city of Alexandria in Egypt. By the time young American doctors or lawyers are hanging out their shingles, Alexander had conquered most of the ancient world. Ivan the Terrible was a boy of seventeen when he forced his nobles to crown him czar of all the Russians. The Battle of Crecy was won by a sixteen-year-old stripling named the Black Prince. Joan of Arc was only seventeen when her army captured Orleans.

During the Middle Ages, youths ten years old became pages in the households of knights and nobles and were treated as adults. In England they were considered "grown up" as soon as they were apprenticed to a craft or trade. By their fourteenth birthday, girls were either married or working as cooks or waitresses, both adult occupations. Eric Hoffer has pointed out that "nothing in medieval dress distinguished the child from the adult. The moment children could walk and talk, they entered the adult world."

Wild Kids, an interesting study by Frank R. Donovan, reminds us that American boys once entered Boston's Latin School (equivalent to a modern high school) at the age of eight and went on to college at fourteen. Admiral Farragut went to sea as a midshipman at the age of twelve — our Annapolis graduates become midshipmen at twenty-two to twenty-eight.

"Achilles fathered a son when he was fifteen," Donovan claims. "Helen of Troy was twelve when Paris carried her off to be his bride; Daphnis was fifteen and Chloe was thirteen; Juliet was fourteen."[5]

But the young did more than make early marriages. Eric Hoffer says they "acted effectively as members of political parties, creators of business enterprises, advocates of new philosophical doctrines, and leaders of armies. Many of the wars in our history books were fought by teen-agers. There were fourteen-year-old lieutenants in Louis XIV's armies. In one corps his oldest soldier was under eighteen."

Over the years the period of deferred maturity has lengthened. As social conditions improved, some families became able to get along without the earnings of their children. With leisure time and well-filled purses, fathers could afford to send their brightest offspring to college. Usually, it paid off financially and the kids loved it, wearing beanies, joining imitation Greek fraternities, and exercising their unearned independence. Soon they were a breed apart, with a talent for aggravating their elders. In 1904, Dr. G. Stanley Hall, a physician, wrote a thick book about them called *Adolescence*. It confirmed their special status. And it recognized the new period between childhood and adulthood as potential dynamite. The passing years have confirmed the good doctor's judgment. The years have also seen a multiplication of problems that verges on the astronomical.

Some sociologists maintain that young people like the system so much that they run the risk of becoming permanent adolescents. A valedictorian at Amherst is reported to have said, as he received his diploma: "Our parents and our teachers believe in adulthood and maturity. Our wish is to stay as immature as little children."

A *McCalls* magazine article says there are four characteristics of these young "drop outs." (1) They have above average intelligence; (2) They are creative and artistic; (3) They come from broken homes or homes where parents do not get along; (4) They feel unloved and rejected.

At least partially, it seems, the parents are at fault. Today's home provides little work. By and large, chores are a thing of the past. When most people talk about work, they downgrade it with reference to long hours, low pay and short vacations. So average young men and women arrive at college with little experience — unless they come from a farm — and with their image of honest toil considerably tarnished. On the other hand, they are experts on leisure, water skiing, dancing, rock music, rapping, TV watching, etc.

Theodore Roszak, the sociologist who wrote *The Making of a Counter-Culture*, rationalizes: "The adolescents who protest loudest today were the babies who were picked up when they bawled, and the beneficiaries of the permissive child-rearing habits that have become a feature of our postwar society. . . . Their kindergarten fingerpainting was thumbtacked to the living room wall and pridefully displayed as a sample of junior's genius. . . . As adolescents, they got a car of their own, or the use of the family vehicle, with attendant sexual privileges. . . . They passed through school systems riddled by progressive classes which have to do with creativity and self-expression. High school was a lark because nobody expected them to learn any marketable skill.

... Economic security was something they came to take for granted. Finally they learned they could talk back to their home-folks without fear of being thrown out. And the product was a new, uncompromised personality, flawed perhaps by irresponsible ease, but also touched with some outspoken spirit. ..." [6]

Perhaps this is the place to say that most parental faults are inadvertent. Parents do overindulge their children, giving them a profusion of material things. This mistake can be disastrous. I have an actor friend who, having given his son every single item for which he expressed a desire, found that boy confronting him one day, saying, "Dad, I hate you!" When the stunned father recovered enough to ask why, the youth told him, "Because you've given me too much." Without the stabilizing effects of earning one's way, of making decisions, of sweating hard to attain some kind of goal, young people are grievously handicapped.

Another problem that "bugs" youth is parental supervision and control through adolescence. Knowing when to "turn loose" is a puzzling problem for my generation. In the long run, it must be done, but when is the right time? If parents hold on too long, grief, heartbreak, and lifelong wounds may result.

To most adults, copping out seems to be a repellent practice, but it is not necessarily all that bad for I have found that it may have spiritual significance. Sometimes the extreme difficulties in which young people find themselves become God's opportunity, opening up a dialogue. We parents must face a couple of things here: *first,* that a concerted attack is being made on our young by an "enemy" who fights with drugs, pornography and radicalism. *Second,* that young people, no matter how beleaguered or how far gone, *need not be losers.* They can be winners!

I have a friend in Florida whose son dropped out at seventeen. He rebelled against everything his parents stood for. Leaving home, he wandered to California. Broke, lonely, discouraged, and on drugs, he was hitchhiking one day when a truck stopped. Three hippie types were in the cab. When they asked where he was going, he answered, "Nowhere!" "Then get in," they said. They were "Jesus people" and they had stopped because they somehow sensed his need. They took him in, loved him, provided for him, and led him to an experience with Christ. That boy's life was completely transformed. He went back to his parents, married a Christian girl, and is now attending a university. "A new creature in Christ Jesus," he is no longer a loser.

Some young people have rejected us older citizens as leaders and advisors, and with good cause. "You've got us into our longest and most discouraging war," you assert. "You've created a society with so much crime in it that the streets are not safe for decent people. You've let technology run wild until the earth is corrupt and its water so polluted that nobody may be around in another decade. Worse, your institutions do almost nothing to improve matters. So step aside, man, and give us our chance."

Let me talk back for a moment. You say stop war, but you do not tell my generation what to do with those who keep on causing wars. You tell us to get rid of pollution in the environment, but you are not willing to stop smoking or to stop driving your car. And what about the pollution of V.D. which many of you spread — and which may eventually destroy many more people than war?

You demand that we stop the killing in war, but thousands are killed and injured every year by teen-agers driving too fast or under the influence of drugs and drink. And what about those of you who are killing yourselves with alcohol or heroin ODs? You claim that you worry about the population explosion, but illegitimacy among teen-agers rises by the hour. It is easy to knock society's tough problems and then, when no "instant answer" is given, to cop out and sneak back into being an adolescent. One thing we all must learn is that problem solving is tough, demanding all that you are. You don't solve problems by turning on and copping out.

Then what *should* you do? This book is my answer. If you are a young man or young woman hooked on dissent or despair, ready to split, then lend me your attention. My answer concerns your dreams and the element in your make-up called "faith." All that God requires of anyone in taking his first step toward Him and toward total self-fulfillment is faith — faith in His Word that teaches that God loves you and that you were alienated from Him by sin, that Jesus Christ died on the cross for you, that when you make a personal surrender to Him as Lord and Savior He can transform you from the inside out.

I have learned that there is an unexpected yearning within the hearts of many so-called hippies. In Watts and Berkeley, in Sydney and London, in Paris and New York, they have revealed themselves to me and my associates. Their goals often seem obscure. They don't know the meaning of "getting ahead." They live in a haze of romanticism. But when they find Jesus Christ, they discover that life takes on meaning and significance. Satisfactions of which they formerly dreamed become vital and real. They do get high, though not on chemicals. Now their "mind expander" is a personal relationship with Jesus Christ.

As I prepared this chapter, the subject of copping out through drugs was presented in articles in *Look* and in *Listen* magazines. The story in the former tells of a hard-won victory over heroin. Its hero is Jesus Christ. The story in *Listen* is one of tragedy. A railway worker found the corpse of a young man in a boxcar. A letter written to his father was in his pocket, along with an empty pill bottle. The youth had copped out. The tragic essence of his letter was this:

> "Dad, the reason I'm doing this is that dope has ruined my life and taken away my happiness. I could not live in the state of mind I was in.
>
> Please don't hate me too much. I thought I had found truth through what I was doing, but I found out too late that I was tripping out on death. I hope to

God that all the other people taking dope find that out, too, and that they don't learn it too late.

From your son, with love, Rick."

Rick had an alternative, if only he had known it. He could have lived and become a victor, not a loser, if someone somewhere had told him about Jesus Christ. Already it has happened to thousands. Today, it is happening on a scale never known anywhere on earth. *Look* quotes one minister as calling it (from a short perspective perhaps), "The greatest awakening in the history of the church, and . . . kids are leading it. Thousands and thousands of young people — upper-middle-class kids and poor kids and often formerly very spaced-out kids — have obviously found an inner real religion."

The article says that the movement came to the fore in Orange County, California, where an entire motorcycle gang was converted and is now a band of disciples on wheels.

In 1969 our team conducted a crusade there in Anaheim Stadium in Orange County, the home of the California Angels. It was attended by more hippies than any crusade I have ever held. In each of the ten services as many as 3,000 persons came forward to make decisions for Christ, a surprisingly high percentage being hippies. Every night they presented a psychedelic sight as they streamed forward in bell-bottoms, in guru robes, bearded and beaded, long hair flowing to their shoulders, and all in one way or another asking, "What must I do to be saved?"

There was the addict who had started on pot, then sped through LSD and amphetamines, and then went on to heroin. Coming forward, he asked, "Can Jesus really get this monkey off my back? I've tried to kick it cold turkey but nothing works." Receiving Jesus, he was back the next night with a friend in a similar predicament.

There was the teen-age girl with the especially beautiful face. But for her, life was anything but beautiful. Her long, blond hair dangled down over her swinging smock and it in turn draped down over her dragging bell-bottoms. She was barefooted. "This place is filled with love. I can't get over it. Everyone seems to love each other!" Over and over she said it, both before and after receiving Christ. A shoeless guru stood nearby, bushy hair falling down his back to match his cascading beard. "God has been looking for me all my life," he said, "and tonight He finally found me. We should have been hitched up years ago."

This awareness of being lost and the consequent craving for identity in another community of kindred spirits may be the greatest hope of the so-called hippie movement.

Perhaps there is this providence in the "copping out" movement. The lostness it implies opens the door to the One who said: "Ye shall know the truth, and the truth shall make you free" (John 8:32). He also said: "For the Son of man is come to seek and to save that which was lost" (Luke 19:10). And Jesus issued that invitation, not in the Temple, the symbol of the religious establishment, but under a tree in the natural world where drop-outs congregate today.

7
HANGING LOOSE

As I travel the youth scene in the early seventies, I find three principal kinds of tension.

The *first* is between youths and those elders they think are standing in their way as they aspire toward a better life. The battle is thousands of years old. *The Journal of Social Issues* explains "those boys and girls don't want to change the world, just the part into which they will fit. Eventually they get their way." [1]

But the question is: Does this generation of young people have the moral stamina to carry through in case of economic depression or in case of another war? The real tests of this generation have not yet come, but they are on the way!

Jesus Christ was concerned about "carry through." He said that no one contemplating discipleship should leave and then later return to his or her worldly anchorages. He told those who were considering following Him that no man launches into building a superstructure without first sitting down and calculating the cost. To regenerate a society, we ourselves must be regenerated.

The *second* kind of tension is created by young people themselves who don't like any part of the world they will inherit and are seeking to abolish our whole society. Some become radical in the "movement," or just drop out from life. Edgar Z. Friedenberg of the State University of New York at Buffalo has invented this apt metaphor to explain them: "They feel they are locked in the back of a vehicle that has been built to corrupt specifications. It is unsafe at any speed and is being driven by a middle-aged drunk. They don't want to drive. They don't even want to go where the car is going. What they want is to get out while they are still alive. If they succeed they will camp where they happen to be, hoping to make it if they can stay together."[2]

The *third* kind of tension comes from those young people who are hanging loose and playing it cool, disturbed by a biting discontent but testing the winds of change before committing mind, body, or soul. They represent the vast majority of modern youth.

These young people can be found today in all countries. Writes a correspondent who visited Poland, "The young people in this land are just hanging loose; their parents have talked incessantly about war and hatred for the Germans. These young people claim an absolute aversion for war and actually like German people. They talk constantly of the generation gap. Only a tiny minority joins the communist youth organizations, claiming 'it is another world for us. The older people who fought and survived — and manage the political scene — are too different from us.' So they simply settle for indifference."

Another reporter visits Bulgaria and reads in an underground youth paper, *Narodna Mladezh*, of the "Nepukism" (I couldn't care less) which has taken over many of the youth of that country: "Our attitude to school is one of indifference. The Young Communist League? We belong to it, and that is all that can be said; the important thing is to be a 'Nepukist' and avoid becoming involved in anything."

I recently entertained an East European communist official at lunch in Europe. He made an interesting comment. He said there are very few dedicated communists left in Eastern Europe. The only dedicated communists are in the West, he added.

Eric Erickson, the famous psychologist who has been among the most influential psychoanalysts of modern times and author of the prizewinning *Gandhi's Truth*, says that all young people come to a period during their teens which he calls a "psychological moratorium." It may last for months or for years. During it the individual asks himself all kinds of torturing questions, the most common of which is, "Who am I?" Questing, floundering, and summing up all his seasons of play and study and his relationships with his parents and teachers, he tries desperately to "put it all together."

The "strong" individual emerges from this moratorium with an "enlarged sense of self" and the ability to measure up to adult sexual, social, and economic responsibilities. The "weak" one becomes discouraged and is apt to withdraw to the friendlier climate of his own fantasies or to a commune of defeated spirits.

The authors Simons and Winograd have said that this moratorium period is characterized by the "hang loose" ethic. The boy caught cheating at exams is told by his peers to "hang loose." So is the girl who commits immorality or becomes pregnant. So are the students who are pressured by parents to get high grades or to make certain of getting an invitation to the prom. In college a hundred pressures tighten the neck nerves and loosen butterflies in the stomach. " 'Hang loose' and you won't be hurt. Don't care all that much and you will be secure," runs the credo. But is it really good enough to deserve universal adoption? Is it really preparing one's growing ego to fulfill itself, or is it "chickening out" on reality?

You "hang loose" by first adopting a way of thinking that rejects commitment to the establishment. For many this rejection includes parents (but not their financial support). It includes God and the notion of earning a living. It asserts the right of all to do their own thing. It applauds the many hippies who ruin their lives with drugs, sex, and fake religion. That's their bag, the cool ones say. It's okay as long as no one hurts anyone else.

If you always "hang loose," the reasoning runs, you can be honest and not be influenced by social pressures.

Simons and Winograd wrote a little book entitled *It's Happening!* which says: "The 'hang loose' ethic is not a uniform thing. One can 'hang loose' happily or bitterly, stoically or desperately, wisely or flounderingly, as a posing actor or a blithe spirit. Sometimes it is mixed with defiance, sometimes with loving tolerance, and sometimes it embodies an indifference that smacks of callous unconcern."[3]

To thumbnail a consensus of what young people have told me and commentators have observed, this style of life involves these various and sometimes contradictory concepts:

(a) When a problem gets rough, "hang loose" and walk away from it.

(b) Don't try to think your way out of a mess, "feel" your way through it.

(c) Accept people the way they are, pimples and all.

(d) Abandon absolute standards; they only hang you up.

(e) Never exploit another person; never be cruel.

(f) Turn up the volume high. Don't listen to music, feel it.

(g) Grow your own tree! Which means studying the subjects that you want to study, obeying the home rules that you want to obey — like running your whole life, man, guided only by your quivering senses.

(h) Distrust tradition and institutions, but have faith in people.

(i) Carry your life in your hand or in a gunnysack or a duffle bag. Accumulate no property and don't worry about bread. Making time payments, reducing a mortgage, or paying a church pledge are a drag.

I have dwelt on this ideology because I want you to understand yourselves. But most of all, I want my generation to understand you. We are idealists too and have been tempted to drop out and "hang loose" thousands of times, but instead we have held onto our jobs, paid our bills, saved our money, and sent you to college. Perhaps we have been naive, but we have expected that you in turn would pick up society's load. So we find it difficult to adjust to your policy of disengagement. Our experience teaches us that problems don't go away. They must be faced, attacked, solved, and then solved again.

Watching the spread of the "hang loose" ethic around the world, we occasionally wonder if your search for reality isn't a cop-out. And, if it goes on much longer, we will ask in bewilderment: Who is going to mind the store? Who will do the work? Who will manage things? Who will defend the country when it is attacked? Who will protect your freedom to live the way you want to? Who will provide the clothes you wear, the food you eat, the clean water you drink, the medical attention, and the thousand other things you depend on if everyone "hangs loose" and drops out? Who will man the rescue squads, the police force, the fire stations?

If the danger appears to be improbable at the moment, then listen to this famous sociologist:

"In remote valleys and canyons or cluttered city apart-ment houses, thousands of young adults, seeking economic advantages, social revolution, love, pot, God, or themselves, are creating a new life style in America.

"Whether the arrangement is called a commune, a colony, a cooperative, an affinity group, or a family, these young adults have some form of sharing in common, and they reject the traditional style of living that groups people together largely because of blood or legal relationships."

As many as two or three thousand of these communes have been reported, says the *New York Times*. Albert Solnit, Chief of Advance Planning for California's Marin County, anticipates that his area will soon have "a city of 20,000 for those who wish to live communally." The communes, he says, are a "new kind of social frontier for the disaffected. . . . Instead of claiming new lands, as the pioneers of the 1800s did, they are claiming new human relationships. Just as the pioneers left established settlements behind, so these communicants have left established ties of family, marriage, class, race, occupation, or anything else that boxes one in." They are trying to "hang loose," but in time they actually become "up-tight" with hang-ups that have no cure apart from God.

Is this the wave of the future or is it a fad? Few think it will last. It has few real, permanent values. Claude Levi-Straus, the learned French ethnologist, is typical of concerned authorities. "They are very poetic . . . but of necessity they retain a sort of game quality . . ." he says of the communards. "They can only be made by a tiny minority shielded and protected, whether it likes it or not, by the strongly structured society which surrounds it. It is precisely this protection which enables the dissident minority to exercise its freedom."

People who live in these communes and sociologists and psychologists who have studied them say that things start out well at first, but then human nature takes over. Psychological problems develop, jealousy rears its ugly head, and they find that human nature is the same in the commune as it was on the outside.

Even a cursory glance at dissenting young people reveals that by the early seventies, the mix in some areas was beginning to sour. Student groups that had been content to parade with flowers in their hair split into noisy factions. Some declared themselves in favor of outright violence: revolutionaries with whom we will deal next. Others were dulled and destroyed by drugs. Some of the fiery student leaders of the sixties are already mental and physical wrecks due to drugs and disease.

Others were jolted out of their "hanging loose" by conversion to Jesus Christ. They decided to "hang in" there in the game of life with the prospect of a sure win on the basis of the Biblical promise, "Thanks be unto God who always causes us to triumph in Christ." Thousands of them have learned the secret of life. They have learned that joy, peace, and love are the fruits of God's Spirit. They have found complete fulfillment in Him. As a result of this commitment, they are taking up their responsibilities of life. They are facing reality and joyously winning others to Christ.

8

WE WANNA REVOLUTION

Unfortunately all of those who "hang loose" and then commit themselves do not commit themselves to Jesus Christ. But the committed are a distinctive body apart from the uncommitted and form another segment of today's youth. As one youth puts it, "Committed, you win or lose. In the game of life who digs a tie?"

"Hang loose" people reckon that the groovy life is one in which all are tied. They are neutralists. "The revolution" people prefer to win or lose. They have decided upon a cause. They may still suffer from confusion, frustration, and fragmentation, but they welcome rivalry. Competition is the grist in the mill of doing their thing. Some may be Trotskyites, Maoists, or Leninists; some may be just plain radicals or anarchists who are despised by others of the far left; they may be members of the new far right organizations which are springing up, especially in Europe; or they may be Christians who are fully committed to their revolutionary goals.

"We wanna revolution!" sang the Beatles in the late sixties, and the vogue of revolution was on for millions around the world. For some it was for real; for some, as John Lennon recently pointed out, it was a game, an escape from reality, a lark. Revolution was the "in" thing. To be "with it," youth had to join the band, to swing with the Jefferson Airplanes as they celebrated rioting in the streets, as they yelled, "Got a revolution!"

History has a message for those who are young today. Someone has written that a people who do not know history are bound to repeat history's mistakes. Your generation needs to know your times and other times. Is today's furious ferment really so different from that of other periods? As far back as one thousand years ago, 50,000 teen-agers ran away from home in a single year to fight for a cause which they had embraced. Historians call it the Children's Crusade.

For over a hundred years, popes, preachers, kings, and nobles had proclaimed a holy war against the Turks who held Jerusalem with its sepulchre in which Jesus had been buried. For two hundred years the war waxed and waned, favoring the Christians and then the Moslems. Millions of Frenchmen, Germans, and Englishmen, among other nationalities, joined a succession of crusading armies, usually to fight and die.

About midway in this conflict — the year was 1212 — a German boy named Nicolas, aged twelve, appeared in Cologne and announced that he had been ordained by God to lead an expedition to liberate the Holy Land. About the same time a French shepherd lad named Stephen, aged twelve, proclaimed an identical mission. Overnight each child became famous as a prophet and preacher, and the word spread that these crusades were surely God's work. The German rallying point was Cologne, and the French gathered at St. Denis, north of Paris. Young Nicolas is said to have led 20,000 adolescents into Italy. Young Stephen rallied 30,000 juveniles and marched them toward the port of Marseilles, promising that the sea would part and provide a dry land route across the Mediterranean. Parents protested in vain.

"Bolts and bars could not hold the children," says Frank R. Donovan in his sociological study *Wild Kids*. "If shut up, they broke through the doors and windows and rushed, deaf to appeals of mothers and fathers, to take their places in the procession which they saw passing by."[1]

The children who marched into Italy simply vanished.

When Stephen's army of 30,000 children reached Marseilles, they rushed to the sea to watch its waters divide. Nothing happened. The promised miracle was a hoax. Hungry and maddened, the youngsters spread through the city like wolves, pillaging, looting, and mugging. Finally two local merchants herded them into seven companies and promised to ship them to the Holy Land. Embarking on seven vessels, the fleet set out. Silence followed, and more years of silence.

Eighteen summers passed, and finally a priest who had accompanied them returned to tell his story. Two of the ships had been wrecked, losing all hands. The five remaining vessels had sailed on to Algerian and Egyptian ports where the children were handed over to waiting slave traders. The good-hearted merchants of Marseilles had been decoys. Sold into slavery and dispersed all over the Saracen empire, the children were never heard from again.

As a society we are much concerned about student demands for a significant role in the management of our universities. In some places they have asked to participate in the selection of faculty members and in the choice of subjects. Often the public has been outraged. We need to read history again. Student participation in university administration is older than any schoolhouse. During the Middle Ages one of the world's first colleges was founded in the Italian city of Bologna by wealthy youths who hired their own professors and selected their own subjects. Having paid their fees, they assumed full command of their classes. Each period was started and stopped exactly on time. Each course was taught according to a prearranged program, and no segment could be skipped by an indulgent or lazy master. If a professor wanted to leave for a weekend, he had to deposit a substantial sum of money to guarantee his return.

When affluence began to spread across Europe, popular teachers set up their own establishments. Often they and their students lived together in abandoned buildings, existing on whatever they could beg, borrow, and steal. When their presence aroused local opposition, they moved to the next city. Eventually several masters with dependable followings came together and created Europe's first university.

A rage to be free and equal has consumed young men and women as far back as the wellsprings of history.

One hundred and fifty years ago, the English poet William Blake wrote,

> Rouse up, O young men of the New Age!
> Set your forehead against the ignorant hirelings.
> For we have hirelings in the camp, in the court,
> And the university, who would, if they could,
> Forever depress mental and prolong corporeal wars.

His summons to the youth of his generation was typical of the nineteenth century when youth became passionately intolerant of political and social injustices. Napoleon's Young Guard, becoming impatient with the suffering of the French peasantry during the French Revolution, demanded a restoration of law and order. One generation later Young Germans laid the groundwork of democracy, rationalism, and socialism. To the south, Mazzini organized Young Italy under the banner of "liberty, equality, and fraternity" — similar to youth's ideals today. With differing objectives but comparable enthusiasm, before the end of the century, Young Europe, Young Ireland, Young England, Young Turkey, and Young America — in that order — were mobilized and on the march in behalf of freedom, prosperity, and equality. Lenin called on Russian youth in 1905 when he was plotting the Communist takeover.

"Go to the youth," he told fellow conspirators. "Make the rounds of hundreds of workers' and student study circles, and supply each group with brief and simple recipes for making bombs. . . . Some may undertake to kill a spy or blow up a police station, others to raid a bank to confiscate money for the insurrection. Let every group learn, if only by beating up policemen."

In this century young people have been used both to save and destroy nations. Adolph Hitler built his new Germany on a foundation of teen-age Nazis by capturing the hearts of young people with his "strength through joy" program. China's Red Guard, mostly teen-agers, turned China upside down. Castro was able to seize the imagination of Cuban youth and lead them into a revolution. Today, youth is again on the march, possessing power unknown in the last century.

In the late 1960s a small covey of irreconcilables followed Abbie Hoffman and Jerry Rubin into a noisy, violence-prone Youth International Party. Newsmen named them "yippies," and the public immediately confused them with peace-loving hippies. Their "thing" was mockery of the establishment, public obscenity, and violent confrontation — such as the 1968 Democratic Convention in Chicago. They set a new style in "trashing." They were among the activists who persuaded hundreds of young men to burn their draft cards. Though they demonstrate furiously today, they apparently do not expect to start a revolution but rather to reveal the idiocy of U.S. life-styles by public education. So they invent publicity stunts to drive home their points. Typically, they reached a TV audience of millions in 1970 when they invaded a David Frost program in London and squirted the star with soda water, smashed scenery, and mouthed obscenities.

The really radical student — would you believe it? — began as an idealist. Whereas the original hippie protested the way in which his own life was "trashed" by society, young radicals became concerned "with society's effects upon others." In this wise, Norman F. Cantor's *Age of Innocence* describes the New Left which spawned the Students for Democratic Society (SDS) which bred the Weathermen faction, among others. And both the FBI and the Communists planted their agents in all these groups.

Often, these dissidents were among the best students at the best universities, places like Berkeley, Wisconsin, Columbia, and Michigan. Most of them came from middle-class homes. All of them were confused and frustrated.

I once asked a student, "What is the difference between

the Old Left and the New Left?" He replied, "The Old Left was a bunch of intellectuals without commitment. The New Left is personal, activist, and deeply committed to change. We'll get things done."

I asked another "burn-it-all-down" advocate, "When you've destroyed everything, what will you do to keep society going?" He answered, "Oh, we haven't got that far yet." He was an anarchist — a breed that even the Communists despise, but are willing to use to serve their purposes.

Are these radicals really the spearhead of a second American revolution? I question it, and so do most sociologists, for the reason that America has no radical class of citizens big enough and discontented enough to rebel. However, the wild ones are not giving up. Sociologist Roszak says, "I am aware that an ideological drift toward righteous violence is on the increase among the young, primarily under the influence of the Black Powerites and a romanticized conception of guerrilla warfare." And he adds, "The original idealism threatens to give way to the politics of militancy, hatred, vindictiveness, and indignation. . . . Suddenly the measure of conviction is the efficiency with which one can get into a fist fight with the nearest cop at hand."[2]

So the young activist drifts in and out of radical organizations, according to his latest ideological bent. Opposition to the Vietnam war bound activists together for a while, but presently they began to fight among themselves. "The radical, left-wing student movement is collapsing into fragmented, embittered, competing organizations, according to a survey of 50 colleges and universities made by the League for Industrial Democracy" and reported by the *New York Times* late in 1970.

At their best, these youthful idealists have impressed me with their devotion to the principles of social democracy and by their conviction that racial discrimination is wrong, that racial prejudice is evil. They desperately want to influence those affairs that affect their lives. They want to change conditions that cause suffering. They want people to be open and honest. They demonstrate against injustice and corruption. They perceive a moral vacuum in the United States and seek to fill it. They support a democratic government, but they want to participate in it. Their politics call for decentralization and humanization. Their background is Camus, not Stalin.

At their worst, young radicals put their personal desires above those of the majority, defy the authorities, and try to turn universities into political battlegrounds. Their hero is the violent man who does the wrong thing to achieve what he calls the right end. Some mistaken groups have adopted names associated with Christianity, church hymns, and an ersatz Jesus Christ in order to advance their cause. Some even copy "the Jesus look" and use marijuana as a religious opiate. As one observer puts it, "Opiates have become the religion of the people." One group in California, adopting an old Leninist device, has named 1974 as the year when they will take over the nation, and, at the latest, they intend to control America by our two hundredth birthday in 1976.

Potentially, they are capable of great harm. For the moment they are diffused by their disunity, by the vigilance of college administrations, and by the sane enterprise of normal, sensible students who comprise the great majority. To further oppose them, right-wing groups are rising in Germany, Italy, Japan, and even in America. Their political beliefs are ultraconservative. In Italy they are called neo-Fascists. Many are Spartan in their demand for personal incorruptibility. They demand law and order under police protection. Only time will tell how effective they will become.

More moderate groups and individuals also are beginning to exert a significant influence on campuses and among young people that far outweighs their number. I recall a story of a single Columbia University student. Grabbing a bull horn during the Columbia riots, he placed himself between an advancing radical mob and the building they meant to occupy. Arguing, explaining, joking, joshing, he talked them into calling off their attack.

The Associated Press recently ran a picture of a football player from San Diego State who guarded the American flag as a group of young radicals were trying to haul it down. Millions of Americans and thousands of fellow students applauded his actions.

Anyone writing about student power must mention *the uncommitted*. On campus they comprise the true Silent Majority, and they are courted by every splinter group and propagandized with "facts," atrocity tales, bullying, and plans for the future. They -- the "uncommitted millions" hold the key to the future. Remember, there never has been and never can be instant justice, instant well-being, or instant peace. But there can be instant decision which can change the course of your life. Zaccheus, the hated tax collector, was instantly converted when he met Christ, as were many others.

Eugene R. Methvin, author of *The Riot Makers*, after studying dozens of student confrontations, finds a powerful swing toward moderation. In *Reader's Digest* he says: "At the University of California at Berkeley . . . moderates formed a Non-violent Action Party and swept 1970's campus elections, defeating a radical coalition by a three-to-one margin.

"At the University of Florida, after continuing sit-ins and disorders by radicals, a twenty-five-year-old law student campaigned for student government president on a platform of more campus police to preserve order. In a field of five candidates he won with fifty-three percent of the vote.

"The spring of 1970, the anti-extremist group at UCLA and San Fernando State launched a United Student Alliance with embryonic chapters on twenty campuses. They raised enough money to open a Washington office and finance training programs for key leaders."

At Penn State moderates formed a Student Committee

for a Responsible University. At Columbia the very effective moderating group was called "Students for Columbia University." In the hysteria following the Kent State killings, when many colleges announced shutdowns, it took the conservative organization, Young Americans for Freedom, "just one day to get court orders reopening classes in three New York area colleges," Methvin says.

From the beginning dissent has been a part of our system. But when it turns to violence, it creates a chaos that the public will not tolerate.

Today strong voices are beginning to be heard representing those students who wish to move the nation forward by utilizing spiritual forces. This option does exist. Thousands of young men and women are aware of it and have dedicated themselves to it.

Frank Barnett says, "In the age of the anti-hero, there (has) emerged . . . a new breed of hero who neither seeks nor needs 'high visibility.' This sort of hero commits himself. . . ."

But I would ask one question of these modern, young reformers: Is your belief firmly based? Is it anchored in a faith that can withstand emotionalism, the drug culture, social and peer pressure, and material temptations? The world is seething with demonic energy. Only supreme inner strength can resist its ceaseless hassling.

Our government accepts the premise that there is always a majority and a minority, and that the latter is duty-bound to try to convert its opponents to a new way of thinking. The history of American progress parallels the making of new majorities. When a minority becomes a majority, a nation renews itself, advancing its services to meet new needs.

Jesus Christ said the gate that leads to destruction is wide and the way is broad, but the gate which leads to life is straight and the way narrow. He was the greatest of all revolutionaries, and He seeks true revolutionaries today who have been transformed by the power of His Gospel and who are prepared to row against the mainstream, to go through the straight gate and follow the narrow way. This way may be filled with suffering, hardships, ridicule, and ostracism from the group. It is difficult to follow Jesus Christ. The problem of applying His teachings to our lives is often confusing; that is why it is so important to rely upon the Scripture and upon the Holy Spirit. In later chapters we will discuss this.

Do you really "wanna revolution"? Are you *that* committed? Then consider the example of Charlie Potter of Reading, England. In his youth he saw many features in society that he detested, and he became increasingly angry. Finally he became a militant Communist and eventually the head of his party in the County of Berkshire. Tirelessly he devoted every spare hour to spreading Communism in Britain.

Then in the spring of 1954 he came to Harringay Arena where we were conducting a crusade, and he heard the claims of the greatest Revolutionary who ever lived, Jesus Christ. Coming forward immediately, he became as dedicated an advocate of Christianity as he had been of Communism.

Bright, radiant, fulfilled, and always at it, he became an evangelist for Jesus Christ to the end of his days when he literally "burned out" in service. All over Great Britain, when he came to town, people would say of Charlie Potter, as it was said of the early Christian apostles, "These that have turned the world upside down are come hither."

Like the Lord he served and the early Christians he imitated, he was a true revolutionary.

9
CONFRONTING THE IDENTITY CRISIS

A confrontation is a meeting. It denotes a conflict between opposing forces, which is precisely what happens when one first confronts Jesus Christ — when the sinner confronts the Savior.

Without this meeting, no one becomes a true Christian.

Confrontation is the special business of young people. They confront their parents, peers, society, law enforcement officers, and themselves, but primarily they confront God. "No creature has any cover from the sight of God; everything lies naked and exposed before the eyes of Him with whom we have to do." Pilate's question, "What then shall I do with Jesus which is called Christ?" is life's ultimate confrontation.

The young confront the evils they find in society, and their searching questions are embarrassing my generation:

— Why are so many people still poor in affluent America?
— Why do ghettos exist in the greatest land in the world?
— Why do racial tensions continue to mount, even though we have the most extensive and far-reaching civil rights laws in the history of the human race?
— Why, with all our talk about national unity, are we still so divided?
— Why, with all our new sexual freedom and knowledge, are we more frustrated, confused, and obsessed with sex than ever?

— Why, with all our investments in security, both personal and national, are we so insecure?

Finally, they ask, "Why are such calamities possible?"

They are possible, I believe, because my generation adheres to five illusions.

The FIRST illusion is that happiness through entertainment gimmicks is the most important thing in life; that America with all its diversionary facilities is the utopia of happiness.

Alexander Klein hits the nail on the head: "Telling the young that the United States has the highest standard of living in the world and that it has the most individual freedom of any mass society is no consolation. It only deepens the despair, reminds them there is no truly just society they can look to anywhere, and suggests that humanness may simply not be adequate to save us. And youth has neither other-worldly nor secular faith to turn to."[1]

The SECOND illusion is that money and possessions bring happiness.

Adlai Stevenson once commented upon this obsession, quoting a significant verse from the Bible: "And he gave them their request," the psalmist wrote, "but sent leanness into their soul." Are we in danger of becoming a nation without a soul?

The THIRD illusion is that permanent peace is just around the corner — and that man, without God, can bring it about.

We fought World War I, World War II, the Korean war, and have recently been involved in a strange war in Indochina; we are told that each war was fought to preserve peace. We have had scores of peace conferences across the world. Still there is no peace.

With all the studies through the centuries concerning peace, our leaders still have not pinpointed the root cause of war. The Bible states it clearly and simply: "From whence come wars and fightings among you? come they not hence, even of your lusts that war in your members?" (James 4:1). As long as men have lust and greed and hate in their hearts, there will be fighting and killing and warfare.

The FOURTH *illusion is the belief that man is naturally good.*

I wish that were true. Our news media demonstrate otherwise. Each day we read and hear stories of such villainy and corruption that we must conclude that something is basically wrong with man. Indeed the Bible teaches: "All have rebelled against God and all fall short of God's glorious ideal." As we have already seen, man has a basic flaw in his nature. It is actually a disease more deadly than cancer. The Bible calls it "sin," "iniquity," "falling short," the "breaking of the moral law."

As Dr. Sherwood E. Wirt has aptly illustrated: "Providing man with more pay, better living quarters, and medical care will not solve his basic problem, for the simple reason that he wants more. He wants his neighbor's pay as well as his own; he wants his neighbor's house and his wife, too. In short, he wants all he can get — power, dominion, glory, and the worship of those around him."

Yet many people still cling to the notion that man is naturally good. We did not get this from the Greeks. Aristotle said: "There is no good in mankind." We did not get it from Judaism. Jeremiah said: "The heart is deceitful above all things, and desperately wicked: who can know it?" (Jeremiah 17:9). We did not get it from Christian teachings. The Apostle Paul said: "All have sinned, and come short of the glory of God" (Romans 3:23).

We got this illusion, I believe, from the philosophers and psychologists of the nineteenth and early twentieth centuries who taught the false doctrine that man is a helpless victim of his environment.

The Bible says that man is not naturally good. All human

experience confirms it. Man is rebellious by nature. The first rebellion in history happened in the Garden of Eden where the environment was perfect and there was no heredity on which to blame it!

Our FIFTH *illusion is that religion without personal commitment and involvement is enough.*

You may be surprised to know that I do not quarrel with Karl Marx's statement that "religion is the opiate of the people." When I talk to university students, I never try to defend religion. Religion has spawned wars. Many so-called religious people have been characterized by prejudice, pride, bickering, and even tolerance for slavery.

However, I would call you to a simple faith in Jesus, who said: "Love your neighbor as yourself."

With much of society a disappointment, young people have begun to search for answers on their own. Everywhere I travel I find young people who are asking: What is truth? Who says so? What is right and what is wrong? Is there a final authority?

Yes! There is an *authority!* There *is* a moral law! It has been exemplified in a real Person. There is a genuine Hero in whom you can believe who will never let you down. His name is Jesus Christ. He was born into a world as jumbled and riddled with injustice as yours, but He changed it by changing people.

Are you really concerned? If you are, I challenge you to take the first step. I challenge you to look at yourself.

You ask: Why not look at the world? Because that mistake has already been made too many times. Let me offer a suggestion.

I ask you to look at yourself, stripping away all ego and pretense. Forget for the moment exacerbations of your government, school, and parents and answer this: "Am I the kind of person on whom a better society can be built? Am I the kind of person who would be good enough to enter the utopia called heaven that Jesus talked about — where all is absolute holiness and goodness?" Your answer, and mine, would have to be "No." We are not good enough. We need a righteousness, a goodness, a holiness that is beyond our grasp. This is what Jesus Christ came to give us.

Experts have told us that society is sick. Their panaceas have treated human frailty with infusions of low-income housing, welfare payments, integrated education, and psychological conditioning. But we are learning that this is not the total answer. The world does need changing, society needs changing, the nation needs changing, but we are never going to change it until we ourselves are changed. And we are never going to change until we look into the mirror of our own soul and face with candor what we really are inside. Then freely acknowledge that there is a defect in human nature, a built-in waywardness that comes from man's natural rebellion against God.

I am not preaching now, just trying to give you an understanding of the modern rationale of what makes you tick. But I also expect to show you that, in the end, you can find your answers only in a personal relationship with God.

Living in a secularized world, most student advisors and counselors deal entirely in secular or godless advice. They may do their best for you, but it is not enough. I have tremendous respect for psychiatrists and psychologists, but even they often cannot answer your queries with authority.

Modern psychology says that you started life as a self-centered being. Some scholars believe that you must remain that way for the rest of your life. Jose Ortega y Gasset holds that "each one of us is interested in self whether he wishes it or not, whether he thinks himself important or not. . . . No one can live my life for me; I must go on living it on my own exclusive account, savoring its gaieties, draining its lees, enduring its sorrows, burning with its enthusiasms."[2]

Strange as it may seem, this is exactly what the Bible teaches. It is interesting that so much of the philosophy of young people, the findings of modern psychology, and many of the statements by modern philosophers agree with the

Bible even though they may be totally ignorant of Biblical teachings.

At a certain age a child begins to undergo physiological and psychological changes. This affects his intellect. Consciously or unconsciously he struggles to discover his true nature and identity. These years, called adolescence, fall between puberty and maturity. Edgar Z. Friedenberg sees this awkward period as a time for seeking "self-definition." "Adolescence is the period during which a young person learns who he is and what he really feels.... It is the age at which he becomes a person in his own right.... A successful initiation leads to group solidarity and a warm sense of belonging; a successful adolescence adds to these a profound sense of self — of one's own personality."[3] In short, you discover and accept the qualities of body and mind that are the real you!

A girl from Radcliffe came home for Christmas and cried for two days. Finally her father got an explanation out of her. She said, "Daddy, I want something, and I don't know what it is." This sums up modern youth; eternally searching, they are not quite certain what they want.

Day after day, they alternate between abysmal hang-ups and fanatical commitments. Psychologists call their malady an "identity crisis." The condition is chronic. Its chief symptom is the cry: "Who am I?"

It is significant that our first astronauts, while being trained for their moon flights, were required to give twenty answers to the query, "Who are you?" Take the same test yourself: "When you have made your list and run out of things to add, ask yourself if you have truly answered? Do you really know who you are?"

Scientists agree that our desperate search leads all humans to seek heroes and to imitate others, to "paste bits and pieces of other people on ourselves." We make love as some actor would. We play golf in Jack Nicklaus style. Part of this process is natural, for we learn by imitating others. The tragedy comes when we realize we have never assembled a true person.

"Who am I?" you cry as you roam the world looking for yourself.

One boy told me, "I have lost my faith."

I said, "No, you have lost your parents' faith. Go out and get a faith of your own."

Your personal faith begins when you resolve: I will face myself now, my problems, my hang-ups, my assets, my faults. Now — right now! — I turn myself over to God. I know that He will accept me as I am because of Jesus Christ.

"Who am I to God?" Here is the modern question. The answer is the essence of the new faith of millions of young people who have seen their lives refocused.

Consider this: There are three of you. There is the person *you* think you are. There is the person *others* think you are. There is the person *God knows you are* and *can be* through Christ.

Over the years hundreds have told me of their fears, hopes, and frustrations. In consultations and rap sessions in college dorms, frat and sorority houses they have voiced their distaste for the rat race for higher grades, of competition for entrance into a "first choice" college, and the manipulations required for status and popularity. They have charged that their parents reject them, that professors treat them as if they were IBM cards, that society refuses to give them a chance to participate democratically in a world they find full of violence, and that adults are hypocrites.

Answering, I have said this: "You are ineffective, and you will continue to be ineffective because you are trying to change the home, the school, the government, and the society without changing yourself. You will never succeed on your own. Idealists in many generations have tried to shape a better world through education, humanitarianism, science, and giveaway poverty programs. All have failed. The individual must be changed."

Many leaders are beginning to agree that the prime problem is man, not society. In *Zen Diary* the philosopher Wittgenstein is quoted by Professor Paul Wienpahl of the University of California as saying: "We, not the world or language, have to be straightened out. The problem is a spiritual one."[4] Many psychiatrists concur.

Yet man persists in waywardness. If one institution fails, try another — anything but God's plan.

I am reminded of a period when all the agonies that afflict modern minds were felt by another generation, the young people who lived during the first century after Christ. They too sought change, but they directed their efforts at individuals, not at the Roman Empire, not at City Hall. And eventually the whole social and political structure felt their impact.

In short, those renewed men and women became filled with a unique dynamic force. Today, this same force is available to all young people. Over the centuries, it has worked in the lives of millions. I, personally, have seen thousands of people changed. Jesus called it "a new birth." The Scripture tells us that you need not continue as you are. You can become a new person. Whatever your hang-up — guilt, anxiety, fear, hatred — God can handle it.

Can you experience this new birth? Can you be born again? Can you start afresh? Nicodemus asked this same question of Jesus one night two thousand years ago.

Being born again means much more than merely a fresh start or turning over a new leaf or making a resolution. The Bible teaches that your old nature is a "self nature." It is incapable of being renovated. You cannot patch it up. Jesus said that cleansing only the outside of the cup leaves the inside as foul as ever. Being born again is the work of the Holy Spirit. God requires that you repent of your sins and receive Christ by faith. The Bible says, "But as many as *received* him, to *them* gave he power to become the sons of God." The Bible teaches that the new birth is an infusion of divine life into the human soul. It is God coming to live within your heart and giving you a new nature. Christ, through the Holy Spirit, takes up residence in your heart. From that moment on you are attached to God forever. Once you are born again, you will live as long as God lives because you will be sharing His very life.

Some time ago I went to a resort city where thousands of college students had gathered during spring vacation. A platform had been built on the beach, and young people, most of them in bathing suits, gathered around by the thousands. I heard the sound of distant surf and the hum of their voices singing songs from the Beatles and Dylan, from Simon and Garfunkel, from Peter, Paul, and Mary — each an evangelist in his own way. The Dylan music was questioning Vietnam — how many deaths are too many? Simon and Garfunkel were offering a bridge over troubled waters. It was a great outpouring of what all too often lies hidden from the "over thirties."

Troubled waters! Troubled times! And a troubled generation. Those young people seemed to be so absorbed in each other that I wondered if they would listen to me. As I started to speak, I hardly knew what to expect. I began by telling them that God loved them, that He would always love them, and that He was willing to accept them into His Kingdom whenever they were ready. The beach became as quiet as a cathedral. They were listening!

And I thought to myself, "Someone has failed them. Who is it? The government? The home? The school? The church? Who?"

Since then I have received overwhelming evidence that their rebellion is not against true faith. It is not against Christ, not against God, nor against any genuine spiritual experience. Rather, it is against the pinch and pressure of a secular and materialistic society.

On almost every campus and in every community you now can find young, committed Christians. And their numbers are swelling rapidly. They are the ones who have decided irrevocably to give their lives to Jesus Christ. They are to be found in a score of youth organizations, in hundreds of youth groups, and in thousands of churches. They have all found God.

A long-haired blonde from a Southern university seemed to be enjoying a satisfactory student career when her grades began to slip. "Life had become one long case of the blahs," she confessed later. "I wasn't walking around with a steady load of the blues, but I sure wasn't enjoying life. Small things made me blow up. I'd met some kids who seemed to know something I didn't know, but I couldn't get in on it. We went to several meetings and one night the speaker said that we don't earn God's love. He takes us as we are. It was then I realized it wasn't a matter of clocking up a certain number of hours doing good deeds. Instead I had to make myself available. Through faith I had to let Him take over. It came together all at once when I accepted Christ as my personal Savior. I know now that God is in me in everything I do. My life is different. It has taken on a new dimension."

Does your life have this new dimension? It can! Just begin now with Jesus Christ! When you make this beginning, it will be your first step toward realizing personal fulfillment, meaning, and joy.

I urge you, have a confrontation with yourself. Admit that you are a moral failure — a sinner — and that you need a new birth. Then have a confrontation with Jesus Christ. Join the army of young people throughout the world who have found a flag to follow, a song to sing, and a cause for commitment. Join the "Jesus generation" and find your true identity in Him.

10
JESUS CHRIST SUPERSTAR

Our generation cannot escape Christ. Throughout the world thousands of young people are talking about Him. A Broadway play entitled *Godspell* is a musical version of Matthew's Gospel. A new movie has just been released, *Brother John,* in which Sidney Poitier plays Jesus Christ in the form of an Alabama black man. The cover story of a *Life* magazine in 1971 was on the rock opera from England, *Jesus Christ Superstar.* This opera confronts young people with the question "Who is Jesus Christ?" It is an eighty-seven-minute electronic probe of the Person of Christ. The opera concludes with the voice of Judas coming back from the dead and still questioning "Who *is* Jesus?" "Don't get me wrong," he says. "I only want to know." And then these haunting words follow, "Jesus Christ Superstar, do you think you are what they say you are?"

Today's youth are looking for a leader. All revolutions, it seems, create a Cromwell, a Napoleon, a Lenin, a Hitler, a Mao Tse-tung, a Castro, a Che Guevara, or a Ho Chi Minh, each of whom casts a charismatic spell over his followers. There seems to be that mystique about them, that real or supposed capacity for getting miraculous things done. That spell is what makes revolution so attractive to some, so repulsive to others.

Human nature, it seems, demands a messiah to follow, to

believe in, and even to worship. God has put that instinct in man so he can believe in the true Messiah who came to save the people from their sins. And that true Messiah is Jesus Christ! He is a true Revolutionary. Revolution means change. He is a changer, changing the lives of all who receive and follow Him.

After visiting dozens of universities around the world, after talking with hundreds of students, I am more certain than ever that young people are yearning today for a "messiah," a leader they can trust and worship. It is not always the God of the organized churches for whom they are looking — certainly not a white God or a black God — but one who identifies with the whole human race; a God who is above and below and *within;* a comforter in time of trouble and a rock in time of doubt. The evidence is everywhere.

I find it in youth's second language, rock music. I find it in the "false messiahs" to whom people are giving their emotions and their wills. We picked up our newspapers some time ago and read how Charles Manson had come out of prison in 1967 and cast his spell over several young people so that they "gave up everything and decided to follow him." This is how a "false Christ" can so capture and dominate the consciousness of his disciples that their wills, activities, and destinies become his.

Each young person has a messiah, whether he knows it or not. The crucial question is: Who is your messiah? The school song of Russian children is "Lenin is always with me," extolling the idea of his being omnipresent with each devoted young Communist. In China thirty million young Red Guards sing the praise of Mao Tse-tung as their creator, savior, ever-present guide, and eternal perpetuator. It is a familiar ploy. Years ago I met an African prime minister who claimed that he was the Lord Christ. In his daily newspaper, he asserted that he was neither from the left nor from the right but from *above:* the messiah of Africa.

"Jesus Christ Superstar, are you really who you say you

are?" Millions of youth seeking a messiah are asking the same question.

Now I don't particularly like the rock opera *Jesus Christ Superstar* because it treats Christ irreverently and perhaps sacrilegiously. But its fatal flaw is that it doesn't go far enough — it leaves Christ in the grave. And without the Resurrection there is no Christianity, no forgiveness, no faith, no hope — nothing but a hoax. However, it has the merit of posing the primary question confronting today's youth. Over and over again it asks, "Who are you, who are you, who are you, who are you, Jesus Christ Superstar?"

Jesus once asked His disciples, "Whom do men say that I, the Son of man, am?" The cover story of *Time* in the spring of 1971 was right when it stated that Jesus Christ Superstar needs to be examined again for what He really is. Today young people are doing just that.

"Where is Jesus Christ?" Innumerable students are re-studying Him and deciding whether or not Christ and the Gospel really matter — whether He is relevant in this modern age. C. S. Lewis, a professor of Medieval and Renaissance Literature at Oxford and later at Cambridge, had to do the same thing. He spent his life exploring the great literature of centuries. In his remarkable autobiography, *Surprised by Joy*, he tells of his pilgrimage from atheism to Christianity. His turning point came with the realization that the writing with the deepest meaning and greatest content was based on a deep, personal faith in God, by men like St. Augustine, Blaise Pascal, George Macdonald, etc.

History, philosophy, theology, and in many centers of learning even the sciences are being studied to discover what they have to say about Jesus Christ. The records of the Early Church are being reexamined for their testimony to Him. Archaeologists are digging to discover new evidence. Some say that Jesus Christ is a myth, that He never really existed in history. Others say that He was merely a man, that there was nothing supernatural about His birth, and that His resurrection was an hallucination. Others talk about a Christless Christianity. Some say that no matter what one thinks about Christ, it does not affect Christianity.

They are wrong! Christianity is forever linked with the Person of Christ. Carlyle recognized this when he said: "Had this doctrine of the deity of Christ been lost, Christianity would have vanished like a dream." The great historian Lecky remarks: "Christianity is not a system of morals; it is the worship of a Person."

Currently Christianity is being compared with other religions as never before. Some so-called Christian leaders even advocate the working out of a system of morals, ethics, and religion that would bring together all the religions of the world. It cannot be done. Jesus Christ is unique.

Why insist on the uniqueness of Christ? What did Christ bring into the world that had not appeared before? The Christian answer is that He is the supreme manifestation of God. "God was in Christ, reconciling the world unto himself" (2 Corinthians 5:19). This is the eternal fact of our Christian faith.

Some seven hundred years before Christ was born, Isaiah the prophet said: "Behold, a virgin shall conceive, and bear a son" (Isaiah 7:14). This expression is unparalleled in literature. In all history, no man but Christ could say that his mother was a virgin. The Scriptures teach that Jesus Christ did not have a human father. If He had had a human father — "that which is born of the flesh is flesh" (John 3:6) — he would have inherited all the sins and the infirmities that all men have. He would have been conceived in sin and "shaped in iniquity," even as the rest of us. Instead, He was not conceived by natural means but by the Holy Spirit, who overshadowed the Virgin Mary; Christ stands as the one man who came forth pure from the hand of God. He could stand before all of His fellowmen and say: "Which of you convicts me of sin?" (John 8:46 RSV). He was the only man since Adam who could say: "I am pure."

There are mysteries about the Incarnation that none of us can ever understand. In fact, Paul speaks of "God . . .

manifest in the flesh" as a "mystery" (1 Timothy 3:16). In another epistle he says: "Let this mind be in you, which was also in Christ Jesus: Who, being in the form of God, thought it not robbery to be equal with God: But made himself of no reputation, and took upon him the form of a servant, and was made in the likeness of men" (Philippians 2:5-7).

From beginning to end the New Testament testifies to the deity of Jesus Christ. The Apostle Thomas addressed Him as "My Lord and my God" (John 20:28). Since Thomas was not rebuked by Jesus, this is equivalent to an assertion on His own part of His claim to deity. He possesses all the attributes of God Himself.

He has divine life. "In him was life" (John 1:4). "I am . . . the life" (John 14:6).

He is unchanging. "Jesus Christ the same yesterday, and today, and for ever" (Hebrews 13:8).

He is the truth. "I am . . . the truth" (John 14:6).

He is holy. "We know that you are the Holy One of God" (John 6:69 NEB).

He existed before time began. "Before Abraham was, I am" (John 8:58). "He is before all things" (Colossians 1:17).

He knew all things. "He knew all men . . . he knew what was in man" (John 2:24-25).

To Him are ascribed all the works of God. "All things were made by him" (John 1:3).

To Him was given worship and honor accorded only to deity. "Let all the angels of God worship him" (Hebrews 1:6). "That at the name of Jesus every knee should bow . . . and that every tongue should confess that Jesus Christ is Lord" (Philippians 2:10-11).

Jesus calls Himself the Son of God twice in John's gospel in chapters 9:37 and 10:30. He does it again in Mark 14:61-62, as well as in many other places either by direct statement or inference. His contemporaries also claimed it. In fact, that was one of the charges brought against Him by His enemies.

When the New Testament prescribes saving faith, it identifies that faith with the deity of Christ. At the conclusion of John's gospel, the apostle says: "But these are written, that ye might believe that Jesus is the Christ, the Son of God; and that believing ye might have life through his name" (John 20:31).

Two things are most important at this point:

First, the object of human faith is Jesus Christ. Over and over it is specified that "Jesus is the Christ, the Son of God." This is the highest revelation of Jesus. Anything less than this level of faith is ineffectual.

The object of faith is not a body of truth called a creed, although creeds are important. The object of faith is a person — Jesus Christ. This is not merely the historical person known as Jesus Christ, but the prehistorical and posthistorical person of Jesus Christ known as the Son of God! He is "the same yesterday, and today, and for ever" (Hebrews 13:8).

We must "by faith" accept Christ as the Son of the living God. This sounds narrow and intolerant, and in a sense it is! Some of our modern theologians would not go so far. In my long study of the Bible, however, I have come to the conclusion that the Scriptures teach that we must *believe* that Jesus is the Christ, the Son of the living God.

When Jesus returned to His home in Nazareth, it is said: "And he did not many mighty works there because of their unbelief" (Matthew 13:58). What was their unbelief? They believed that Joseph was His father, that He was not the Son of God.

Salvation is an act of God. It is initiated by God, wrought by God, and sustained by God. The faith that saves the soul is described as faith in Christ as the Son of God — not as a good man or a great man, but as the uniquely begotten Son of the living God! This is consistent with the witness of the entire New Testament and with the proclamations of the first preachers of the Gospel. All proclaim the necessity of faith in Jesus Christ as deity.

The second important thing is that the effect of faith in Jesus Christ is "life." "And that believing ye might have life through his name." And what is "life"? The Bible describes man as alive physically but dead spiritually. A dead man needs life. The whole human race is said to be "dead in trespasses and sins" (Ephesians 2:1). This means they are dead to God. They are incapable of generating divine life. Only God can do this. Man is capable only of believing and receiving. The "life" spoken of is that with which Adam was created, but which he lost because he sinned. It is this "life" that Jesus possessed as the eternal Son of God. It is this "life" that was subjected in the wilderness temptation to the enticements of lust and to pride. It is this "life" that undergirds our daily existence today, as demonstrated by Christ who was "in all points tempted like as we are, yet (was) without sin" (Hebrews 4:15). This "life" became available to all humanity through Christ's death on the cross. He said: "I am come that they might have life" (John 10: 10). This is the "life" you can have; this is Christ in you, the hope of glory.

The human life of Jesus has been praised by the greatest of men. Many brilliant minds have recognized Him as the world's unique and superlative character. Their estimates have testified to His historic reality and have confirmed that what He was and did are based on fact. Rousseau said: "It would have been a greater miracle to invent such a life as Christ's than to be it." Another has said: "It would take a Jesus to forge a Jesus." Pascal wrote: "We know God only by Jesus Christ. Without this mediator all communion with God is taken away; through Jesus Christ we know God." Men are truly awed by Him. No natural explanation is adequate. He can be ranked neither with school-trained scholars nor with self-trained wise men. Yet, He spoke as one who *knows* the truth and *is* the truth. As Philip Schaff said: "Christ stands . . . solitary and alone among all the heroes of history, and presents to us an unsolvable problem, unless we admit Him to be more than man, even the eternal Son of God."

Thus all of Christianity is based on a person — Jesus Christ. He is the embodiment of the Gospel. He makes the highest claims with no sense of pride, ambition, or vanity, but with the simplicity and authority of self-evident truth. And when Jesus spoke to His own generation, He said: "If ye believe not that I am he, ye shall die in your sins" (John 8:24).

Christ represents Himself as having been "sent from God" and being "not of this world" and having "come from God." He declares Himself to be "the light of the world," "the way, the truth, and the life," and "the resurrection and the life." He promises eternal life to everyone who believes in Him as the Savior. When in view of His approaching death, and under a solemn appeal to the living God, He was challenged by a religious leader: "Art thou the Christ the Son of God?" He answered in the affirmative. Referring to His return, in His moment of deepest humiliation, He proclaimed Himself the divine ruler and judge of all mankind (Matthew 26: 63-65).

Such overwhelming testimony leaves us with the conviction that Jesus was not merely a good man or a great prophet, but the Son of God, divine as well as human, revealing in His life and by His teaching the mind and heart of God. Indeed, it is the *deity* of Christ, above anything else, which gives to Christianity its sanction, authority, and power.

Ultimately, every human being must face this question: What do you think of Christ? Whose Son is He? We must answer this question with belief and action. We must not only believe something about Jesus, but we must *do* something about Him. We must accept Him or reject Him.

Jesus made clear who He was and why He came into the world. In His own lifetime He asked His disciples: "Whom do men say that I the Son of man am?" Whereupon Peter replied with his historic affirmation: "Thou art the Christ, the Son of the living God" (Matthew 16:13-16). This is the apex of faith! This is where every man's faith must rest if he hopes for salvation. Eventually, you too must decide "what shall I do with Christ?"

What a Messiah to lead a revolution!

"Put your hand in the hand of the Man from Galilee!" The words come from millions of loudspeakers. Rock bands chant, "He's coming down to get you. Are you ready?" Jesus said: "Be ye therefore ready also: for the Son of man cometh at an hour when ye think not" (Luke 12:40).

A college girl tells this story: "School and social life didn't fulfill my inner needs as I had expected them to. I left school to search elsewhere." She tried Confucianism, but its three thousand points of behavior were a bit too much. She sampled Zen-Buddhism but found it even more difficult. Friends assured her that true freedom could be achieved chemically. She tried various drugs and felt the trap of addiction closing. Unable to stop, she began to despise herself. She was in despair when she received an invitation to attend a conference of young Christians. She finished her story in these words:

"I met people there who had the love and peace in their hearts that I had always wanted. They said the answer to my search was Jesus Christ. Through them I learned how to take Him into my heart and trust Him with my life. Then the change began. It came about almost in spite of me. Certainly it was not my own doing because I didn't have the strength. Yet I began to know inner peace and the reality of God's love. With Jesus deep in my heart, at last I had a purpose for living and for giving. Finally, for the first time in my life I experienced the elation of being wholly free, of being a fulfilled individual."

Have you met Jesus Christ?

He can be *your* Superstar! He can be *your* Lord! He can be *your* Savior!

Life's greatest tragedy would be to miss Jesus Christ.

11
TURNING ON

We get dirt off our bodies by turning on the water in the shower. We get the darkness out of a room by turning on the light. We get our automobiles to run by turning on the switch. The "hip" generation popularized the phrase "turning on" to describe the drug experience. Smoking pot, dropping acid, or shooting heroin, they turned on for a high and got into their trip.

To become a Christian, you must "turn on" to God by placing your full faith in Christ as Savior and confessing Him as Lord. And the wonderful thing about it is that it works.

I once conducted a crusade in a city that was having one crisis after another with its restless young people. One night I disguised myself and attended a rock festival in order to discover what attracted so many — thousands. Next day, I reported that I had been present and publicly invited the entire hippie set to attend our services. They responded by the hundreds, and when I invited them to receive Christ, scores came forward. Recently, one of them wrote to me.

"I came to the crusade because I thought you were a regular guy," he said. "To those of us who attended it was to be just another experience, something to relieve our boredom. But as you spoke, I began to hear another voice, and I knew that what you were saying was 'truth.' When you asked us to come forward if we wanted to receive Christ, I rose almost spontaneously and walked down the aisle! Standing there, I felt more alive than I'd ever felt in my life. Everything I had searched for or longed for seemed to materialize in that one moment. I stayed on with my old friends a few more weeks, but presently I gravitated to those who had shared my spiritual experience. All of us began to pray regularly and to study the Bible. I am now attending seminary, studying for the ministry. I expect to spend the rest of my life spreading the thrilling news of God's love and forgiveness with all that will listen."

This young man had been "born again." He had been "turned on" spiritually. "Without intense and intimate personal feeling, you never learn any valuable truths whatever about life," Josiah Royce said recently in *Time.* Jesus Christ works like that, channeling His revolutionary power into the lives of those who put their faith in Him. He talked frequently about drastic changes, but always they had to start in the heart. This is why He insisted on conversion and new birth. "Verily I say unto you, Except ye be converted, and become as little children," He said, "ye shall not enter into the kingdom of heaven" (Matthew 18:3).

The shape of things to come has been apparent in our crusades for several years now, as a vast majority of our audiences included more and more young people, and as many thousands of them have marched across football stadiums and down the aisles of great indoor arenas to discover a new life. Their identity crisis is over! They have found what they were looking for by turning on to Jesus.

Young people not only need conversion; they *must* be converted if they are to find God. In his book about youth, *The Making of a Counter-Culture,* Theodore Roszak stresses the importance of "visionary experience," insisting that this is more relevant to an integrated life than mere technical brilliance. Only when man "refuses to block, to screen out, to set aside, to discount the needs his own personality thrusts upon him"[1] will he discover himself.

His conclusion? "It is my conviction that those who open themselves in this way and who allow what is 'out there' to enter them and to shake them to their very foundations are not apt to finish by placing a particularly high value on scientific or technical progress." ... (and) "Where and when the lightning will strike that unaccountably sets one's life afire ... is beyond prediction."

Surely he is talking about (from a psychological point of view) what Jesus called conversion. About giving "what is out there" a chance to enter in. About changing the person. Roszak does not call this Christianity, but he has borrowed it from Christianity.

Not long after my own conversion, I read a tract entitled "Four Things God Wants You to Know." Campus Crusade for Christ, which has played a major role in sparking the new "Jesus Revolution," has expanded these four items into a beautiful little booklet and given them away by the hundreds of thousands. Literally, it has helped countless young people to get "turned on" spiritually.

The first law is that God loves you and has a wonderful plan for your life. God loves you! Most young people have heard or perhaps memorized John 3:16, the most familiar verse in the Bible. In one modern version it reads: "For God loved the world so much that He gave His only Son so that everyone who believes in Him should not be lost, but should have eternal life."

Young people talk a lot about love. Most of their songs are about love. "All You Need Is Love," "I Can't Live in a World Without Love," "The Glory of Love," "Man Without Love," "Love Can Make the Poorest Man a Millionaire" are recent examples.

"The supreme happiness of life," Victor Hugo said long ago, "is the conviction that we are loved." "Love is the first requirement for mental health," declared Sigmund Freud. The Bible teaches that "God is love" and that God loves you. To realize that is of paramount importance. Nothing else matters so much.

And loving you, God has a wonderful plan for your life. Who else could plan and guide your life so well? He the Shepherd; you, one of His sheep. A young woman who came forward in one of our meetings told us how God had once seemed so far away; but now, in Jesus Christ, He was always near at hand in every situation. "The will of Christ for me," she exclaimed, "is wonderfully simple and simply wonderful."

The second spiritual law is that you must acknowledge you are a sinner — by nature and by practice. This sinful nature separates you from God and makes it impossible for you to experience either His love or His plan for your life. David, the great king of Israel, once wrote: "I was shaped in iniquity and in sin did my mother conceive me." Isaiah the prophet expressed the same idea, "All we like sheep have gone astray. We have turned everyone to his own way." Solomon, one of the wisest men who ever lived, explained that man's instinctive behavior, when he excludes God, is invariably disastrous. "There is a way that seemeth right unto man, but the end thereof are the ways of death." Jesus made it clear that the easy, popular way is the wrong way, "Wide is the gate and broad is the way that leadeth to destruction and many (the majority) there be that go in thereat." But "straight is the gate and narrow is the way that leadeth into life and few there are that find it" (Matthew 7:13, 14). Paul argued to the Romans that the defilement of the human race was universal. "They have all gone out of the way" and "the way of peace have they not known . . . for all have sinned and come short of the glory of God." Not only does our sin make us come short of God's expectations, but it separates us from God. Isaiah taught, "Your sins have separated His face from you."

Youth senses this guilt, this alienation, this separation from God, and wonders what causes it. A reader wrote to "Dear Abby": "When a kid goes wrong, which factor is more responsible, his heredity or his environment?" Abby replied, "It's a toss-up." The Bible says exactly that! We are sinners both by heredity and environment; both by nature and by nurture; both by instinct and by practice.

In the book *Man's Search for Meaning*, Viktor Frankl describes his experiences in the Nazi concentration camps of

Auschwitz and Dachau, where men from the same backgrounds and in the same environment behaved differently; some acted like swine, others like saints. Frankl says it is a matter of choice. Man chooses how he will react, how he will behave.

Because we *are* sinners, we often feel lonely, and unloved. A social scientist once polled the people of this country and discovered that at any time during the day about 135,000 Americans are saying, "I'm sick and tired of everything!" In his first chapter, the prophet Isaiah described the sins of ancient Israel and noted the results: "The whole head is sick and the whole heart is faint." Look around! Listen to youth today. The Rolling Stones have made "I Can't Get No Satisfaction!" one of the most popular modern songs. The title speaks for itself. Sin brings no satisfaction. Inger Stevens won the Golden Globe Award as the best televised actress during the sixties and began the seventies by taking her own life. "Sometimes I get so lonely I could scream," she had said. That's alienation! The feeling is shared by the youth of every country in the world.

So why not quit beating around the bush! Why not call our problem by its real name, which is "sin." Sin is selfishness — it's a transgression of God's laws — it's coming short of God's moral requirements — and of these we are *all guilty*. Let's face it, admit it, and forsake it! That is called repentance. Jesus said, "Except ye repent, ye shall all likewise perish." That word repentance is used in the New Testament more than seventy times.

The third spiritual law is that Jesus Christ is God's only provision for man's sin. Only through Him can you know and experience God's love, forgiveness, salvation, and plan for you. "For at the very time when we were still sinners, then Christ died for the wicked," wrote Paul. John said, "In this was manifest the love of God toward us that the Father sent the Son to be the Saviour of the world." Jesus did not say that He was *a* way. He said: "I am *the* Way, *the* Truth, and *the* Life; no man comes to the Father but by me!"

Sometimes we miss the significance of the cross on which Jesus died, stumbling over its simplicity. Its uncomplicated meaning is that Jesus Christ has paid the price of our sins. By taking our place and our punishment, He gave us the gift of forgiveness, cleansing, and everlasting life.

Recently I read that it will cost this country a hundred billion dollars to get one man safely to Mars. It cost God the priceless blood of His only Son to get us sinners to heaven. By tasting death for every man, Jesus took over our penalty as He erased our guilt. Now God can forgive. In a moment of thanksgiving, Paul once exclaimed: "He loved me and gave himself for me!" Will you repeat these words right now, even as you read. If you do, I believe you will have cause to be thankful, too, and that you will experience the love of God in your heart. Try it and see. The Bible teaches that you can be absolutely sure that you are saved. The Apostle John wrote: "These things have I written unto you that believe, that you may *know* that you have eternal life."

All the religions of the world are simply men looking for God. But Christianity is not merely one more religion. In Christianity, God is searching *for* man — and revealing Himself *to* man. That is why God has placed in man's heart a restlessness and a frustration — until he finds God! God's search for man led to the cross where His only Son suffered and died — died for you. This sounds foolish to modern ears. And to the ancients as well. When Paul went to the pagan city of Corinth, he said: "The proclamation of the cross is foolishness unto them that perish." But then he added: "The foolishness of God is wiser than men and the weakness of God is stronger than men" (1 Corinthians 1:25). In that ancient city, the cross of Christ was a stumbling block to the Jews, and to the Gentiles it was idiocy. Intellectual Corinthians preferred a system of philosophy predicated on the ability of man's mind to unravel the divine. They wanted something their minds could grasp. So Paul tells us that "the natural man receiveth not (cannot understand) the things of God" (1 Corinthians 2:14). Nor must you understand all God's mysteries in order to find Him and receive Him and know Him. A doctor writes a prescription which we cannot read for the treatment of a disease that we do not understand, and we gladly pay a sum which may seem unreasonable because we rely on his knowledge and have faith that he will make us well. Before the cross can have any meaning at all, the Spirit of God must open the mind. So long as we remain separated from God, the Scriptures teach, our minds are covered by a veil. To such a one — to an "outsider" — the cross must appear as a ridiculous symbol. To those of us who have experienced its transforming power, however, it represents the only cure for sin — the basic ill of humanity. The cross is the focal point of the life and ministry of Jesus Christ. His death upon it was no afterthought with God. When Christ took our places, our sin was laid on Him — and sin cannot be in two places at the same time. My sin was laid on Christ and, therefore, I have no sin charged to me. My sin is now Christ's burden. He has taken its load off me. He has become the sin bearer. Though I was indebted to God, Jesus paid off my debts. I will never suffer the shame of judgment or the terrors of hell. "As far as the east is from the west," said the psalmist, "so far hath he removed our transgressions from us" (Psalm 103:12).

Do you remember the train load of poison gas that became a national issue? It was in danger of leaking, and the big question was: where could it be safely deposited. Finally they hauled it out into the Atlantic and sank it. Each of us carries a load of sin more poisonous than any gas. We ignore it as long as we can, but eventually it begins to leak. We try to drown our awareness of it with drugs, alcohol, or frenzied activity. We try to unload it on friends, clergymen, or psychiatrists. There is only one safe depository — it is at the cross of Jesus Christ, the only place where sins can be totally blotted out without poisoning others.

Are you saying, "I don't understand any of this. It sounds ridiculous!" Listen! If a man were drowning and I threw him a life belt, would he say, "I'll not put this belt on until I know whether it's made of rubber or cork or if the material is strong enough to hold me"? No man in danger of drowning talks like that. No man who is ignorant of Christ is capable of comprehending the mystery of the cross as long as he is separated from God.

The Bible says that God was in Christ reconciling the world unto Himself. You are a part of that world. God wants you to be reconciled to Him — and He has provided a way in the person of Jesus.

The fourth spiritual law requires that you must openly accept Christ as your Savior and Lord. Only then can you know and experience God's love and plan for you.

Throughout one's youth, one struggles constantly to be "accepted." We want to be accepted by our parents, by our teachers, by our peers, and by our girl friend or boyfriend. To gain this acceptance, you will do almost anything. In the beginning of the letter written to the Ephesians, Paul exults in the fact that, as believers, God has "destined us — such is His will and pleasure — to be accepted as His sons through Jesus Christ." Think of it — sinners such as you and I *accepted* by God! As His son! No wonder John Newton, the slave trader, after his conversion wrote, "Amazing grace, that could save a wretch like me."

To "turn on" spiritually, you need only to open your heart to Jesus Christ and ask Him to come in. He says: "Here I stand knocking at the door; if anyone hears My voice and opens the door, I will come in and sit down to supper with him and he with Me." How beautiful! How simple! How thrilling!

My own heart was empty once. Fortunately I asked the right question and got the right answer. "How does one get the help he needs? How can I find God?" For me, the answer came from an older friend.

"Repent of your sins, ask for forgiveness, and receive by faith Jesus as the Son of God as your Lord and Savior.

Do that and God will accept you," he said. It has not changed through the years.

We are supposed to do more than admire Jesus. We are to "put Him on." As Paul wrote to the Ephesians, "Put on the new nature . . . created after the likeness of God in true righteousness and holiness! The likeness to God that we had at the first, the likeness that we lost by sin, is created again in us when our lives are joined to Christ."

Paul the apostle often spoke of the Christian as being "in Christ."

That is a Christian person's true identity.

Having done this, now I know my past — it is sinful but forgiven — and where I came from; I came from God. I know what went wrong; I tried to play God instead of being satisfied to be a real man. I know my future; my destiny is Heaven. And I know the present; I live in the here and now having Jesus always within me, His Holy Spirit to guide, teach, and lead.

Leighton Ford often concludes his sermon on finding yourself with this question: "Will the *real you* please stand up and find your identity in Jesus?"

Many letters come to me from young people who have given their lives to Jesus Christ, telling of signs and wonders. "I was voted the most popular girl and the girl with the best personality," Karen writes. "But underneath all the glory and my seemingly adjusted personality, I was searching. Something was missing. One day after school, a young math teacher told me that every human being needs to have a personal relationship with God through His Son Jesus Christ.

"I had thought that I was a Christian. Then it hit me that there's a big difference between knowing *about* Jesus and knowing Him personally. In a very unemotional way, I asked Jesus to come and live in my heart. Now my life has real happiness, real purpose, and real power as well in it."

Bob, a college student, was a natural-born winner. At a Southern university he became his frat's social chairman. Studying industrial engineering, he made the Dean's list for five straight years and was elected to the top senior leadership honoraries. His chief rule of conduct was "eat, drink and be merry." He enrolled in the Harvard Business School, certain of a brilliant future. When he married a lovely girl, it all seemed too good to be true.

"I agreed with my friends that I had it made," he writes. But his marriage soon collapsed and the bright promise of tomorrow faded. Obviously, fun and games were not enough. Along the way he had met several students who talked of having a personal relationship with Jesus. He recalled, "The only requirement was to ask Christ to come into your life and take control of it," he recalls. "So why not? In the weeks that followed, I began to experience a new kind of joy and peace. As I began to trust Him, I have seen my desires and attitudes change. I have come to understand that real success and happiness can be found only as the result of a continuing day-by-day trust in Jesus Christ."

A young intellectual, a Phi Beta Kappa named Vera, told us her story. She had stopped believing in God during high school. Her views were close to those of Camus and Sartre. At Berkeley, the last wisps of her faith vanished because every subject she studied "seemed to agree that the concept of a personal God was a figment of man's imagination."

About the time of the Free Speech Movement, she had to write a paper that involved the teachings of Jesus Christ. By chance, a Campus Crusade group held a meeting at her sorority house. "I was amazed that those students spoke as if they actually believed that the Bible was the Word of God. My curiosity was awakened," she recalls. Soon she was meeting weekly over coffee with the wife of a director of the religious movement, listening to the novel thought that Christianity was not so much a "religion" as a relationship with a Person. Slowly, she came to admit that Jesus was real, but a personal God was still too big a bite to swallow.

Two months later, she boarded a plane. The aircraft flew through clouds for a while and then soared up into blazing sunshine. "I can't explain what happened," she remembers, "but it was as if a veil were pulled back and I could see beyond. In that instant, God spoke out, saying, 'I am!' The Bible had given me some pieces of the God puzzle, but because I did not have all the pieces, I'd been saying that God did not exist. At last I understood! How ridiculous it was to try to fathom the infinite with a finite mind."

Through the years I have learned that such moments of illumination come to many whose hearts are suddenly opened. Vera's intellect abruptly told her that God existed. Simultaneously, she realized that she must face Christ; that she could live without Him or she could commit her life to Him.

"For a moment, I became as the Bible tells us to — like a little child," she said. "Then I simply said something like, 'All right, Jesus. I give myself to You. Do whatever You want.' And then I felt such a flood of love and such deep peace and joy that I knew things were going to change forever."

Right now, thousands of young people are confronting the living Christ. You can too. Would you like to pray the short prayer we pray in our crusades with those who come forward to receive Christ?

Oh, Lord, I am a sinner. I am sorry for my sins. I am willing to turn from my sins. I receive Jesus Christ as my Lord and Savior. I confess Him as Lord. I want to serve Him from this moment on in the fellowship of His Church. In Christ's name, Amen.

If you have said that prayer with me, then take one further step. Write to me, and I will send you some literature that will help you to recognize your privileges and responsibilities as a new young Christian. Send your letter to: Billy Graham, Minneapolis, Minnesota. That's all the address you need.

12
GETTING HIGH

"Are you supposed to get high and stay there?" a university student asked me. "I've been a Christian for only a few months, but I find that I also have some lows."

You will have wonderful "highs," but you will also experience some "lows." This is normal — and is a part of God's plan. Both "uppers" and "downers," created by your emotions, are part of every human's lot.

What happens to you when you make your commitment to Jesus Christ?

First, your sins are forgiven. "In whom we have redemption through his blood, even the forgiveness of sins" (Colossians 1:14). Throughout the New Testament we are told that the one who receives Christ as Savior also immediately receives, as a gift from God, the forgiveness of sins. Forgiveness is not merely the pardoning of sins but the restoration of a relationship. This means that you are without guilt in God's sight. It means that you stand before God as though you had never committed a sin, cleared of every charge. No matter how high or how low you feel, the Scripture teaches that you have been forgiven.

Second, you are adopted into God's family. As Paul said, "To redeem them that were under the law, that we might receive the adoption of sons" (Galatians 4:5). The moment you receive Christ as Savior, you receive the divine nature of the Son of God. This makes you a joint heir with Christ.

You enjoy all the rights and privileges of a son. All things in God's Kingdom become yours.

Third, the Spirit of God lives in you! Before He ascended into heaven, Jesus Christ said: "And I will pray the Father, and he shall give you another Comforter, that he may abide with you for ever: .Even the Spirit of truth . . . ye know him; for he dwelleth with you, and shall be in you" (John 14:16, 17). During His lifetime, Christ's presence could be experienced by only a small group. Now Christ dwells through His Spirit in the hearts of all who have received Him. The Apostle Paul wrote: "The Spirit of God dwelleth in you" (1 Corinthians 3:16). The Holy Spirit is given to you, not for a limited time, but *forever!* If the hour comes when you feel that the Spirit has abandoned you, don't be discouraged. He is in you *forever.* Accept this fact by faith!

Fourth, because the Spirit resides in you, you now have the prospect of winning daily victories over temptation and sin. "There hath no temptation taken you but such as is common to man: but God is faithful, who will not suffer you to be tempted above that ye are able; but will with the temptation also make a way to escape, that ye may be able to bear it" (1 Corinthians 10:13). The Bible teaches that you are now to "abhor that which is evil" (Romans 12:9) and "Put . . . on the Lord Jesus Christ, and make not provision for the flesh, to fulfill the lusts thereof" (13:14).

But how can you do this? Where do you get such a capacity and such strength? God once said through Ezekiel the prophet, "I will put my spirit within you, and cause you to walk in my statutes" (Ezekiel 36:27). Your victory will come from the Spirit of God within you, never as a result of your own struggles. You need only to believe in and yield to Him to receive His help in resisting sin. Through faith you can become "more than conquerors" (Romans 8: 37). The Bible does not teach that sin will be eradicated, but it does teach that "sin shall no longer reign over you." You are no longer its slave. Its strength and power are broken. Now the Bible teaches that the moment you come to

Christ you become engaged in a *great conflict.* "For the flesh lusteth against the Spirit, and the Spirit against the flesh: and these are contrary the one to the other: so that ye cannot do the things that ye would" (Galatians 5:17). This means that you often will have a conflict within. True, you do possess a new nature, you have been born from above, but the old nature is still there. Now it is up to you to yield to the reign and control of the new nature which is dominated by Christ. The Holy Spirit will help. Before you came to Christ, you practiced sin. In other words, sin was your habit. You were dominated by sin. Now that power has been broken, and the Bible teaches that "whosoever is born of God does not practice sin" (1 John 3:9). You may fall into sin, but you will immediately be sorry. You will hate it. When you, as a Christian, commit a sin, you will be miserable until the sin is confessed and fellowship with God is restored. The difference between the non-Christian and the Christian is that the non-Christian makes sin a practice; the true Christian does not. The latter abhors sin and tries to live by the commands of God with the help of the Holy Spirit. Thus, Paul describes Christians as those "Who walk not after the flesh, but after the Spirit" (Romans 8:4). Again, "Neither yield ye your members as instruments of unrighteousness unto sin: but yield yourselves unto God, as those that are alive from the dead, and your members as instruments of righteousness unto God" (Romans 6:13).

Feed your new nature on the Word of God. Starve your old nature which craves the world and the flesh. And "present your bodies a living sacrifice, holy, acceptable unto God" (Romans 12:1). From now on your choices will be made from a new perspective and in a new dimension. When you live up to the full powers of your new life, sin loses its control.

Under the Lordship of Christ, you will begin to acquire new ideals. Many of your tastes will alter completely, not from conscious effort of your will, but because of the change within you. Some of the things you once did, you will stop doing. Some of the things you once shunned, you will do. For many, this change will come suddenly; for others, it will be a slow transformation of outlook and way of living as you gradually assume the likeness of Christ.

Be aware of the *deceitfulness of your emotions.* Never depend on them for "truth." At times you will feel a "spiritual high." At other times you will feel a "spiritual low." They are part of God's plan, and He may be closer to you during a low. A period of depression may be His way of testing you. He wants you to walk by faith, not by feeling.

David, who was called "a man after God's own heart," had both highs and lows. He once implored, "Let thy salvation, O God, lift me up on high." He was low, but he wanted to be high. Yet he wrote, "Yea, though I walk through the valley of the shadow of death . . . thou art with me; thy rod and thy staff they comfort me" (Psalm 23:4). Samuel the prophet recorded how God "lifted me up on high." Jeremiah told those around him to "set thine heart toward the high way."

The first automobile I ever drove was a Model T Ford. It had no first, second, third, and fourth gears — only low and high. To start, you pushed the left pedal. When you got up enough speed, you moved a lever forward with your left hand and took your left foot off the pedal. That put the car into high. We lived in the country on a muddy road. To get to town on Saturday night, we had to drive out to the highway, turn right, and presently we would be where the action was.

The life of a young Christian has a low and a high, too, with many in-betweens. Thousands of years ago Job prayed: "Set up on high those that be low." The spiritual Model T from which you can learn to "drive" your life is named "trust." "Trust in the Lord with all thine heart." When you turn right toward the destination that God prescribes, you turn off a muddy side road onto a highway of holiness, and you are on your way to where the action is.

But here is a paradox. *It is possible for the young Chris-*

tian to live high while feeling low. God's rivers run deep; they never change. Our circumstances and feelings will change, but God's love, mercy, and grace will never change. The Holy Spirit will never leave our hearts. Paul instructed the Ephesians, "Be filled with the Spirit." I could urge you to stop your bad habits, whether they be dishonesty, drugs, immoral practices, or any other wrong thing on which you are hooked, but unless you are offered a force with an up-draft powerful enough to overcome the downward suction of wrongdoing, it would be useless. Christ offers such a force. It is the Holy Spirit! He provides the only dependable high the world has ever known.

What a pity that this kind of high was apparently unknown to Janis Joplin and Jimi Hendrix. How tragic that their kicks came from a poison that finally extinguished their genius. How regrettable that they never gave their lives fully to Jesus Christ and experienced the kind of high from which one never crashes, the one provided by the Holy Spirit.

A popular song is called "Heaven Everyday." But one cannot have heaven everyday while practicing sin. One of my college classmates wrote the song "Every day with Jesus is sweeter than the day before." The recipe for that kind of joy is to be filled with the Holy Spirit and never to allow an unconfessed sin to persist. You can have constant fellowship with God.

Another good point to remember is that living on a spiritual high begins and continues only through *humility.* You cannot go around with a feeling of self-righteousness. When Peter, James, and John were on the Mount of Transfiguration, Peter was so high and proud of his position that he said, "Lord, let's build three tabernacles, and we'll stay up here. It is good for us to be here." But God Himself gave answer. God said, "This is my beloved son. Hear him!"

Peter had felt: "What a wonderful experience. What a high! Let's stay here forever." An emotional experience had diverted him. God had to bring him down to earth. Peter said, "Lord, it's wonderful." God said, *"He* is wonderful!"

Never underestimate the *danger of being diverted.* You may thrill to some supreme experience, but we are told to be occupied with Jesus Christ Himself. Sin diverts some. Pleasure diverts others. Social service and "religious" activity divert others. We can even become so preoccupied with the amazing gift of the Holy Spirit that we are diverted from His Person. So remember Peter. Remember that God spoke not of the mountaintop scene but of the Person. God said, "Hear *Him!*"

If we are to experience the fullness of the Holy Spirit, if we are to have a true spiritual high, then we must get down low before God. Water always runs to the lowest place to find its level. The way up in the Christian life is down! Paul instructed the Romans, "Be not high-minded." If you would have a spiritual high, get down off any pedestal of pride you may be on. Get down on your knees in prayer, with your Bible open, poring over the Scriptures. Then get up and go out and witness for Him by serving Him.

It is important for you to build your high by *reading and studying the Scriptures.* David said: "Wherewithal shall a young man cleanse his way? By taking heed thereto according to thy word" (Psalm 119:9). And: "Thy word have I hid in mine heart, that I might not sin against thee" (119:11). Satan will try to keep you from reading the Bible. So I challenge you to outwit him by reading and memorizing a portion of the Word of God each day. Failure to do so will cause you to trip up and fall on your face. When Christ was in the wilderness, the devil tempted Him three times. Christ met each temptation by quoting Scripture, saying, "It is written . . ." (Matthew 4). If Jesus Christ found it necessary to thwart Satan's attacks by quoting Scripture, how much more do all men need the help of this mighty weapon.

When the Ocean Group sings "Put Your Hand in the Hand of the Man From Galilee," they are symbolically confessing that they study the "Holy Book" and that what they read makes them "tremble." Jerome, one of the early Christians, said, "Ignorance of the Bible means ignorance of Christ." Job once said, "I have esteemed the words of his mouth more than my necessary food." Jeremiah said, "Thy words were found, and I did eat them; and thy word was unto me the joy and rejoicing of mine heart."

To read the Bible, one needs a "quiet time." Christian students often ask, "How do you maintain your spiritual high? What do you do on a day-to-day basis?" I tell them about my "quiet time." Some days it is in the early, sometimes late morning, sometimes evening. Without it, my Christian life would be a wilderness. Isaiah said: "They that wait upon the Lord shall renew their strength; they shall mount up with wings as eagles; they shall run, and not be weary; and they shall walk, and not faint" (Isaiah 40:31). So gain the strength of eagles, as the prophet suggested. Set a time each day when you can spend a few minutes alone with God.

Job wrote: "Doth the eagle mount up at thy command, and make her nest on high? She dwelleth and abideth on the rock, upon the crag of the rock, and the strong place" (Job 39:27, 28). That nook in the crag's crevice gives the eagle its power as king of birds. Thomas à Kempis, the great saint, said, "I have no nest but in a nook in the Book."

Your own nook, your own "strong place" for achieving a spiritual high can be your daily "quiet time."

Some time ago, the nation heard a radio interview between a well-known disc jockey and a yogi disciple of Hari Krishna. They talked about the importance of transcendental meditation. The articulate guru said that meditating fifteen minutes each day was necessary for peaceful survival. He used this illustration. When a man at an archery range pulls back on his bowstring, one might ask him why he pulls backward when he desires to thrust his arrow forward. His reply would be that the further back he pulls his bowstring without breaking it, the further forward his arrow will go. So, the yogi said, all people need a special time for meditation in order to pull themselves back from the whirlwind that is modern society, and so to gain strength for thrusting their own spirits into God's world.

In my own life, I find that the more I pray, the more I feel the need for knowledge of the Scriptures; and the more I read God's Word to obtain that knowledge, the more I have to pray and the more power I have in prayer. In my own day-to-day schedule, nothing is ever as important to me as my time with God.

Another factor that contributes to a spiritual high is *obedience*. The Scripture says, "God gives the Holy Spirit to them that obey Him." The ancient Israelites needed great courage and faith when they left Egypt. In Exodus 14:8, we read: "Israel went out with a high hand." Only through obedience to God were they able to maintain their spiritual high. From then on, their key word became "obedience." If you want to live in a spiritual high of your own, you must obey implicitly the leadership of God through the Holy Spirit. He [the Spirit] will never lead you contrary to the Word of God. I hear people saying, "The Lord led me to do this. . . . The Lord told me thus and so. . . ." I am always a little suspicious unless what the Lord has said is in keeping with His Word. God never directs us to do anything contrary to His Word. The prophet Samuel once said, "Obedience is better than sacrifice." The Scriptures teach: "He that willeth to do his will shall know the doctrine."

When you find yourself up a blind alley, not knowing which way to turn, if you are willing to do His will, He will reveal Himself. He conceals His will only from those who, before they consent to do His bidding, seek to know what He is going to say. Be an obedient Christian. Remember that where God guides, He provides. Where He leads, He supplies all needs!

Some time ago I received a letter from an invalid in Jacksonville, Florida. This young person, in the midst of troubles that would drag most young people into a deep depression, had found a permanent spiritual high in Christ. "For a long time I have been bitter about life," he wrote. "Ever since I was twelve, I have been waiting for death, for at that age I discovered I had muscular dystrophy. I fought hard against it, but I only grew weaker. All I could think of was what I was missing. My friends went off to college, got married, and began to have families. Lying in my bed, I felt despair creeping from every dark corner.

"Whenever you came on television, I usually watched. When you gave the invitation, I heard nothing. Last year mother brought me your book *World Aflame*. Reading it, I realized that I wanted God. I wanted to find a meaning for my life. Then a strange thing happened. Suddenly, I became aware of an unmistakable assurance that there was a God who loved me. This assurance was so powerful that it led to a deep conviction. Afterwards, I was numb for a week.

"Now my life has changed and I have great joy. My despondency has vanished. My hopes are high. I continue to grow weaker, and I am nearly helpless and in pain most of the time, but I am so grateful that I am alive that it's hard to keep myself from bursting at the seams. At last, I can see the beauty that is all around me, and I realize how lucky I am. Despair is such a waste. Lack of faith is such a waste. Thanks to God, so long as I am here, there is so much I can do."

God promises no easy life or days without troubles, trials, difficulties, and temptations. He never promises that life will be perfect. He does not call His children to a playground, but to a battleground.

Some young people have a warped idea of helping the Christian cause. Seeing talented, brilliant Christians, they attempt to imitate them. For them, the grass on the other side of the fence is always greener. When they discover that their own contributions are more modest or perhaps invisible, they collapse in discouragement and overlook genuine opportunities that are open to them.

Be like the Apostle Paul and say, "None of these things move me." Few men suffered as Paul did, yet he learned how to abound and how to be abased. He learned to live high — even in a prison cell. You can do the same. Refuse to permit circumstances to get you down. In the midst of your difficulties, there will be a deep joy. "For the joy of the Lord is your strength," says the Bible.

Finally, you will experience peace. Paul said, "Troubled on every side, yet not distressed; we are perplexed, but not in despair; persecuted, but not forsaken; cast down, but not destroyed" (2 Corinthians 4:8). All these qualities are characteristic of true Christians. They can be yours, giving you the ultimate victory. They are part of your birthright. Claim them!

As a child of God, you need never suffer spiritual defeat. Your days of defeat are over. From now on, you will want to live every minute to its fullest. Certainly, you will welcome each day as another twenty-four hours to devote to Christ. Every new day will be filled with opportunities to serve others. You will spend many moments with God, and you will know that your sins are forgiven and that you are on the way to heaven.

And that is really "getting high."

13
THE DEVIL IS ALIVE AND KICKING

"Satan is alive and well," according to a recent survey. And it certainly seems evident from the number of articles about the devil that have appeared recently in national magazines. One publication featured thirty-five pages about the devil as he appears in Satan worship, witchcraft, sorcery, spiritistic seances, demonology, wizardry, black magic, yoga masters, psychic seers, poltergeistry, and voodoo priests.

A few years ago, the idea of the existence of the devil had gone out of style along with "fire and brimstone" preaching. Today, while there is a statistical drift from the organized church, an ever-increasing percentage of Americans — now sixty-five percent — believe in a personal devil. At a time when the educational system of our nation has virtually excluded the Bible and God from the classroom, parapsychology has worked its way into the center of the curricula.

Nor is the devil enthroned only in our academic institutions. Churches dedicated to Satan worship are springing up all over the country. Their services include black masses, goat's horns, demon imagery, nudity, and songs lauding Lucifer. The film world has moved from the mere use of such catch titles as "The Devil's Doorway" to themes which actually center around Satan, such as "Rosemary's Baby" (Satan is the father).

And this devilish trend has taken to the streets to propagate Satan worship through psychic music, grabbing rituals, "Process" propagating proclamations, and the aggressive distribution of literature. You meet them on the sidewalks of Seattle, San Francisco, Omaha, Atlanta, Toronto, or New York. On Easter weekend, 1971, 5,000 Satan worshipers gathered in Chicago to celebrate the rise of the devil. Early in 1971, 450 "Ministers of Satan" were "ordained" in one week in a small city in the Northwest.

Satan worship is now a world-wide phenomenon. Recently, a Presbyterian minister in Britain informed me that the occult and witchcraft are even more pronounced there than in America. In England, a nation which many had thought of as perhaps the world's most rational society, a legislator now claims that a majority of the secondary school students have been in touch with either a witch or a wizard. Nor is this phenomenon limited to the West. The *Los Angeles Times* news service has been carrying stories about whole villages in Russia being taken over by witchcraft and wizardry. There is a great revival of Satan worship in Northern Europe, especially in Germany.

The Bible teaches that *the devil and his demons are real.* The word "Satan" comes from the Greek word "diabolos"; the word "devils" or "demons" comes from "diamonia." The Bible teaches that demons are capable of entering and controlling people. They are spoken of as unclean, violent, and malicious. All outside of Christ are in danger of demon possession. The Bible teaches that these demons continue to harass Christians, even after their conversion. "For we wrestle not against flesh and blood, but against principalities, against powers, against the rulers of the darkness of this world, against spiritual wickedness in high places" (Ephesians 6:12).

Jesus and His apostles frequently cast out demons. Peter was addressing "younger men" when he cautioned: ". . . be on the alert! Your enemy the devil, like a roaring lion, prowls around looking for someone to devour. Stand up to him, firm in the faith . . ." (1 Peter 5:8 NEB). James urged us to "Be submissive then to God. Stand up to the devil and he will turn and run" (James 4:7 NEB). Paul taught that the devil is a tricky tactician: ". . . Satan himself masquerades as an angel of light. It is therefore a simple thing for his agents to masquerade as agents of good" (2 Corinthians 11: 14, 15 NEB). He also predicted that as the end of the age approached all this would worsen, reaching a "final rebellion against God when wickedness will be revealed" in "the work of Satan" to "be attended by all the powerful signs and miracles of THE LIE."

So the pressure is on, and the onus of responsibility rests upon you to seek complete victory over the devil in the Lordship of Jesus Christ. The devil has supernatural power but not total power or knowledge. Jesus said, "All power is given unto me in heaven and earth." Satan's power is limited. He can act only under the permissive will of God. There is a mystery to this that no theologian totally understands. Paul called it the "mystery of iniquity."

Satan engages us in spiritual warfare. To understand more about his power and tactics, let's consider the encounter which Jesus had with the maniac of Gadara (Mark 5). For a long time this man had been troubled by demons who had implanted an "unclean spirit" in him. When he was transformed by the power of Christ, it says that he was in his "right mind."

Satan can affect the mind. There is more derangement in the world today than ever before, with millions of Americans struggling to maintain a balanced mind. Could some of this be satanic activity? I think so. This does not mean that everyone who is mentally deranged is possessed by demons. However, I do believe that some of it is Satan, especially in those who have yielded their lives to lust, drugs, alcohol, etc.

The devil will also attack people morally. The maniac whom Christ met in the wilderness wore no clothes. He ran naked through a desolate cemetery. What is it that creates the craze in our day for nudity? Movies and magazines, nudist camps and pop festivals are constantly accentuated by nudity as a life style. This is not new. The maniac of Gadara did it because the devil got into him. He not only tore off his clothing, but also the chains and restraints which were imposed upon him by society. And he abused his body by cutting himself with jagged stones. All this was the work of the devil.

Perhaps you find that you abuse yourself. You don't protect your body which, if you are Christ's, is the temple of the Holy Spirit. Youth who mainline drugs are pushing a self-destruct button. Fornication, Paul says, is sin against your own body. This is true also of gluttony, drunkenness, and smoking. These are slow suicide. The devil promotes anything which tends immediately or ultimately to destroy you.

Mark says that the maniac became *violent*, and this, too, was the work of the devil. Until God chains the devil, man will be hopelessly intimidated by this recurring resort to violence. Man cannot control himself, and if he will not be controlled by Jesus Christ, then he will be controlled by Satan.

We read that this demon-possessed man was compelled to live in a cemetery. He lived with the dead. The Bible teaches that we "were dead in trespasses and sins" (Ephesians 2:1). Your body may be alive, but your soul is dead toward God until you are born from above. However, a wonderful phrase in Psalm 88:5 says, "Free among the dead." When you come to Jesus Christ, He frees you from the dominating power of Satan. While the world around you may be spiritually dead, you can be spiritually free and alive!

We have seen that Satan is a threat. *How does the Christian meet this threat?* By keeping Jesus Christ enthroned in his life as Savior and Lord. Thus he excludes the devil from a place in his life. "Greater is he that is in you, than he that is in the world," promised John. And an ancient Hebrew prophet promised: "When the enemy shall come in like a flood, the spirit of the Lord shall lift up a standard against him." As long as the Christian invokes the Name of Jesus, and insofar as he yields himself fully and constantly to Him and studies the Scriptures, he will enjoy spiritual triumph. "The Son of God," we read in the New Testament, "came to earth with the express purpose of liquidating the devil's activities" (1 John 3:8, Phillips).

A Christian must rely on the Word of God. When Jesus was tempted by the devil, He answered Satan's temptation with: "It is written. . . . " Three of history's most attractive propositions were made by Satan, but each time Jesus replied with, "It is written." God has exalted His Word to be equal to His own Name. Is it any wonder that the devil always retreats in the face of the Word of God? He hates and fears its power.

The Bible teaches that every Christian is tempted, but it also teaches that temptation is not a sin. It is the yielding that is sin. All temptation is from the devil. God will test us, but He will never tempt us to sin! "There hath no temptation taken you but such as is common to man: but God is faithful, who will not suffer you to be tempted above that ye are able; but will with the temptation also make a way to escape, that ye may be able to bear it" (1 Corinthians 10:13).

An illustration I like is of the housewife chasing a mouse with her broom. The mouse wastes no time eyeing the broom — he is looking for a hole. Get your eyes off the temptation and look for the way of escape.

The Bible says we are to *"resist the devil"* and "fight the good fight of faith." You reply, "But the devil does such fascinating things." Yes, we read in the Book of Revelation that there will be "spirits of devils working miracles" and, hence, those who "worship devils." This prophecy is behind much of the current Satan worship. But the Christian is to "resist the devil." Tell him to get off your back.

This can be done through prayer. In our Lord's model prayer, He commanded us to pray daily: "Deliver us from the Evil One" — that is the devil. "We are not ignorant of his devices," said Paul, and Peter spoke of "your adversary the devil." He is always lurking in the shadows and crouching under a nearby bush. And he is rough! In the gospels we read such things as "the devil threw him down"; "when the devil had thrown him in the midst"; a man "was driven of the devil into the wilderness"; and "my daughter is grievously vexed with a devil." Is it any wonder that Martin Luther threw an inkwell at the devil? Hudson Taylor, the great pioneer missionary to China, when asked how one can know there is a devil, suggested, "Resist him for a day and you'll soon find out."

In the final book of the Bible we read that *they overcame him by the blood of the Lamb.*" The reason Jesus came to die on the cross was: "to destroy the works of the devil." When you find yourself unable to triumph over the devil through your own strength, claim your victory in the name of the Lord Jesus.

On a number of occasions in my ministry I have met people in various parts of the world whom I was convinced were demon possessed. Missionaries encounter them frequently. We read of them in the news today. How else can one account for a Hitler or the mass killers of our generation?

And finally we read, *"They overcame him . . . by the word of their testimony."* You cannot maintain an upper hand over the devil unless you are prepared to witness constantly for Christ. Personal witnessing is an integral part of Christian victory. When Jesus had cast the demons out of the maniac of Gadara, the healed Gadarene wanted to go with Him. But Jesus said no. He told him: "Go home to your friends and tell them the great things the Lord has done for you." I would urge you to do the same.

Yes, the devil is alive and kicking. But if you are in Christ and follow the simple rules of daily Bible study, prayer, and witnessing, *he has no power over you!* "In all these things we are more than conquerors through him that loved us" (Romans 8:37).

14
COMMITMENT
AND
INVOLVEMENT

Most of the men whom Jesus called to be His disciples were probably young. They were called to a life of self-lessness, sacrifice, and total commitment. Jesus told them frankly: "Anyone who comes with Me must leave self behind." He also told them: "Whoever wants to be great must be a servant, and whoever would be first must be the willing slave of all — like the Son of man. He did not come to be served, but to serve, and to give His life as a ransom for many."

Jesus didn't use subtlety or gimmicks to gain followers. Rather, He honestly laid before them the tough demands of discipleship — total commitment and total involvement.

I remember when Jim Vaus came forward to give his life to Christ in our Los Angeles Crusade in 1949. Jim was a wiretapper in the underworld, and when he came forward, he was a rich man. But in a few days he owned only the suit of clothes in which he stood. After he had received Christ, he wanted to make things right with those he had wronged, and it took virtually everything he had to make restitution. Later Jim told me that his conversion, before it was finished, resembled the Allied attack on the German/Japanese Axis during World War II. The Allies committed themselves to total invasion and, as the Axis was nearing defeat, demanded unconditional surrender. When the armistice was signed, both of the vanquished, West Germany and Japan, never had it so good. Jim said, "Jesus Christ came at me with total invasion. His terms were unconditional surrender. And when I yielded myself totally to Him, I discovered that I had never had it so good." Jim became a social evangelist in New York City, combining complete commitment to Christ with social involvement.

Christ lays down conditions, but only a few can meet them. Only a few are willing to pay the price. Christ's way is a way of discipline, renunciation, and hardship. The verbs used in the New Testament to describe the Christian life are "fight," "wrestle," "run," "work," "suffer," "endure," "resist," "agonize," "mortify." The Scriptures describe a Christian as a soldier who must suffer hardship. Paul wrote to Timothy: "Thou therefore endure hardness, as a good soldier of Jesus Christ" (2 Timothy 2:3).

In Matthew 16:24 Christ laid down three conditions to His disciples. A disciple is one who puts teaching into action. The word "disciple" actually means "learner." It also carries with it the idea of discipline. Christ said, "If any man *will*." It is a matter of personal choice.

1. *"Let him deny himself."* Self means the flesh, the old man, the natural man. The self-life manifests itself in self-indulgences, such as self-love, self-will, self-seeking, self-pride. To different people it may mean different things. To one man it may be intellect, to another pleasure, to another it may be family. It takes self-denial to turn off the television and spend an hour in prayer. It takes self-denial and discipline to read the Scriptures. It means that all aims and desires are subject to Christ — your career, your boyfriend, your girl friend. The only object in life is that Christ may be honored. Paul said: "But what things were gain to me, those I counted loss for Christ. Yea doubtless, and I count all things but loss for the excellency of the knowledge of Christ Jesus my Lord: for whom I have suffered the loss of all things, and do count them but dung, that I may win Christ" (Philippians 3:7, 8).

2. Christ said, *"Take up his cross."* This is a voluntary action. You have a free choice in the matter. It is not the

cross of punishment for sins; only Christ could carry that. It is not a cross of gold, ivory, or silver that you may wear around your neck. It is not a cross of poverty, sickness, nor loss of friends. It is not the common annoyances and vexations of life. Our burdens are not our crosses, contrary to what many people think. The disciples were startled at Christ's statement. To them the cross was a despised and hateful thing. It was a symbol of Roman torture and shame. It was a place where criminals were executed.

To take up your cross means to associate yourself with Christ and to share His rejection. It means you take a stand for Christ even though people make fun of you, persecute you — or even kill you!

In John 15:19 Jesus says: "If ye were of the world, the world would love his own: but because ye are not of the world, but I have chosen you out of the world, therefore the world hateth you." The moment you receive Christ, you may experience ostracism from certain groups with whom you have associated in the past. For a while you may lead a lonely life until you find a new fellowship with Christian friends. You may be ridiculed, and some may actually be hostile, but to take up your cross means to share the fellowship of His rejection. Paul wrote to young Timothy and said: "All that will live godly in Christ Jesus shall suffer persecution" (2 Timothy 3:12). Surrendering to Christ is like signing your name to a blank check and letting the Lord put in the amount. Commitment means burning all bridges behind you.

3. Then Christ said, *"And follow me."* One of His disciples said: "Lord, allow me first to go and bury my father." Jesus said to him, "Follow me; and let the dead bury the dead" (Matthew 8:21, 22). Even the sacred duty of burying one's own father was not to interfere with the higher obligation of following Christ. Jesus said: "He that loveth father or mother more than me is not worthy of me: and he that loveth son or daughter more than me is not worthy of me (Matthew 10:37).

Are you ready to go this far with Jesus Christ? Are you ready to follow Him in a disciplined life of prayer and Bible reading? Are you willing to follow Him with a disciplined mind and tongue?

One of a Christian's responsibilities in following Christ is to have a new attitude toward work. So many young people want Christ without responsibility. Jesus was not a drop-out. As a carpenter, He worked hard with His hands. The Apostle Paul made tents for a living while he carried on the work that God assigned him. Whatever work a Christian does is done unto the Lord. He should do his best at whatever his trade or vocation. He should be faithful, clean, and honest. As a matter of fact, the Bible teaches that he who does not work should not have the right to eat (2 Thessalonians 3: 10).

The Christian is to dress with neatness and cleanliness. The Bible does not say anything about styles that change from generation to generation or from culture to culture, but it does teach neatness and cleanliness. This is part of the Christian commitment in discipleship.

To follow Christ also means a surrender in the area of social involvement. For example, *drugs*. It is not enough to have been saved from drugs yourself, or even to have had a miraculous conversion which involved kicking the drug habit. Get involved in helping others kick it. The only *real power* to counteract drugs is Jesus Christ. Show them that Christ cares, and provide them with the kind of sacrificial service which a true servant of Jesus should give.

What about *pornography?* Why don't you young Christians do something about the pornography pollution of our time? Twenty million sex-centered magazines litter our newsstands with new numbers each week, each edition trying to escape new laws from the bottom of the sewers. We put lids on our sewer holes. Ought we not to do something about the pornography which is spewing out a polluted river of filth which can destroy us faster than any chemical pollution we seem so worried about?

Joan Winmill Brown is the wife of Bill Brown, President of World Wide Pictures. While in New York City Joan bought groceries from a supermarket where there were piles of hardcore pornography. Once a London actress, she knew both sides of the street. She decided that in Christ's name those piles of obscene literature must go. She got other young customers together and saw the manager. He felt a bit embarrassed about what was on his stands, and his conscience had been hurting. He responded to Joan's crusade and the pornography was moved out. This could happen right across our country.

And the pornographic movies: Millions of Americans are sick of them. But there are too few of us who are doing anything about it. Edmund Burke once said that all it took for evil to triumph was for good men to do nothing.

When we were in New York City for a crusade, the first of the so-called "sex-all-the-way" movies hit 57th Street. Entitled "I am Curious Yellow," it was showing across from Calvary Baptist Church. The young people from Calvary Baptist organized a picket protest against its being shown. One of the placards read: "I Am Furious Red!" There is a righteous indignation against evil. In a Southern city a group of evangelical young people organized to protest the displays of pornographic painting and objects in an arts theater there, and they were able to get an injunction from the courts to close it.

What about *safe driving?* Do you realize that over a thousand people are killed every week on the highways of America, most of it through careless and drunken driving. Highway safety is a crusade in which Christian young people should be engaged. I believe in obeying the speed laws and all the traffic rules. I also believe that those who are out to insure greater safety at the manufacturing and legislating levels ought to have Christian support insofar as they are acting in the interests of society.

Let's allow Christ to restrain us from the wild impulses of

youthful vitality which often overpower normal sanity with the daredevil craze to drive like maniacs.

What about the *race problem?* In spite of the finest civil rights laws on the statute books of the world, racial tension continues. A new separatism is beginning to creep into some of our major northern cities. Far beyond the crusade for civil rights for furthering better race relationships is the need for constant exchange of fraternal rapport between, say, blacks and whites at the family level. The majority of white Christian families in this country have never in their lifetime visited in a black home, and to a lesser degree perhaps, vice versa. Young people can cross a new frontier in this area of race relations by spending time in the homes of people of another race. Your life will be enriched. Those with whom you have fellowship will be enriched, and you will have a real understanding based on actual and constant experience of interracial fellowship.

What about the *dirt, garbage* and *pollution* in your own neighborhood? How dirty is your street? How shabby is your neighborhood? How polluted are the streams around your home?

What about visiting the *lonely?* Under almost every roof lives one or more persons who are lonely, alienated, depressed, wishing that someone would come and pay them a pleasant visit. President Nixon said recently that as an outcome of the decadence of our society, increasingly people are being harassed by alienation, negativism, and defeatism, and they need a moral regeneration. This kind of regeneration is not always going to be effected on your first visit. But social contact and sharing is a beginning.

To the *Los Angeles Times* a woman writes: "I'm so lonely I could die. So alone. . . . I see no human beings. My phone never rings. . . . Did you ever feel sure the world ended? I'm the only one on earth. How else can I feel? All alone. See no one. Hear no one talk. Oh, dear God, help me. Am of sound mind. So lonely, very, very much. I don't know what to do." I think that we Christians sometimes forget that this verse is in the Bible: "Religion that is pure and genuine in the sight of God the Father will show itself by such things as visiting orphans and widows in their distress and keeping oneself uncontaminated by the world" (James 1:25, Phillips).

There are thousands of lonely shut-ins: in homes for the aged; in hospitals for incurables; in wards for the mentally deranged; in jails, prisons, and penitentiaries where you can go to them but they can't come to you. Go and sing to them, or just go in and talk to them. Talk to them about Jesus. But talk to them also about anything and everything which is wholesome. Listen to them. Laugh with them, cry with them, empathize with them, share with them. That is your social privilege. It is your spiritual responsibility. Jesus said: "I was in prison and ye visited me!"

And then there are disasters: fires, earthquakes, landslides, traffic accidents, hurricanes, floods, and crime victims. Don't just watch them on the news or read about them in the papers. So many who have been involved have complained that the only people to turn up are reporters, cameramen, firemen, and doctors. They need you.

I heard about a colony of so-called hippies who were converted to Jesus Christ. Visiting such families in distress became their "thing." A home was robbed. The family was in distress. This group helped them. They prayed with them. But they also secured legal aid for them. This is Christian commitment in action.

What about your *vocation?* There is a tremendous need for Christians in such areas as journalism, medicine, psychology, diplomatic service, and even politics. I heard about a Christian at one of our universities who studied journalism, got a job as a reporter on the student newspaper, and by the time he was a senior he became the editor. Through his leadership in the student paper, he changed the attitudes of an entire campus. This is what I wish many Christian students would do. We have neglected getting involved from the inside.

There is a tremendous need in the field of psychology. More and more people are suffering under the pressures and tensions of modern life, but we have too few Christian psychologists and psychiatrists.

There is a developing shortage of doctors in the United States today. What opportunities a Christian physician has to serve Jesus Christ socially, spiritually, and physically, both at home and throughout the world.

And then there is *politics*: because of the acute pressures morally, intellectually, and economically on politicians today, fewer and fewer of the more qualified men are coming forward to serve. If the trend for statesmen to be replaced by opportunists goes much further, our democracy, with such deep Christian roots, is going to be lost. And apart from running for office, we need young people who are idealists to stand shoulder to shoulder in supporting candidates who will bring real moral integrity, spiritual insight, and intelligence to the increasingly demanding tasks of politics. It is your youthful responsibility as Christians to be constructionists at a time when the ranks of the young have been so heavily infiltrated with destructionists who sometimes just protest, demonstrate, and march for the "kick" they get out of seeing things demolished.

And the *mass media*: before the average high schooler leaves for college he has spent 15,000 hours watching television. You know the crime, war, violence, and sex exploitations which have become so much a part of the feeling and thinking of the average young person today. Why don't you ask God if you ought not to get into journalism and write as a Christian ought to write; or into script writing for radio and television; or into radio or television as a news reporter or analyst. That's where the action is!

And as our world becomes a global village, some of you ought to be thinking of service for Christ in Africa, South America, Asia, and the islands of the sea. Don't let anyone mislead you — *missionaries* are still desperately needed, though not in the same way they were needed fifty years ago. There is not nearly as much need for pioneer missionaries as there used to be, though that need still exists. You might not feel called to preach, but you could be a Bible translator. Over a thousand tongues are still waiting in spiritual need for the translation of the Scriptures. Teachers, nurses, agriculturists, and technicians — they're all so desperately needed on the outposts of the earth. You need to take some action in this direction. This may be the only way Americans can be missionaries in the future.

Finally, it seems to me that one of the neediest areas for young Christians to exert their influence is in the *church* itself. Don't turn the church off! Even though the synagogues of His day were not what they should have been, Jesus went faithfully every Sabbath. The Apostle Paul followed the same example. Wherever he went, he was in the synagogue on the Sabbath. The churches may not be all that they claim to be. They have made many mistakes. There are many hypocrites in the church. However, the church is God's organization upon earth, even with all of its faults and failures. Every Christian young person ought to go faithfully to church to make a contribution as well as to worship.

The polls all indicate that while in essence the Jesus generation is becoming more and more religion conscious, the churches are getting emptier and emptier. Many ministers are discouraged. They would be tremendously encouraged to have a visit from you. You may make suggestions to your pastor concerning forms of worship. Certainly you ought to pray for and encourage him. Be constructive. You can talk to him even about his sermons, if you approach it in the right way. Most of all, encourage him to preach Christ, to preach the Bible, to speak on such subjects as conversion, the New Birth, the Holy Spirit, or the Second Coming of Christ.

There is so much that I would like to say to you who have recently made your commitment to Christ. It's so exciting, thrilling, and adventuresome to follow Christ; to have the answers to the problems, dilemmas, and mysteries of life; to know where you have come from, why you are here, and where you are going; to have found that secret of life for which millions of young people are, consciously or unconsciously, searching. You have found it in a personal relationship with Jesus Christ. But the best is yet to be — as you grow in the grace and knowledge of Christ.

Throughout the length and breadth of your commitment to and involvement in the various phases of your Christian life, keep Paul's suggestion in mind: "That in all things Christ might have the preeminence"; whatever you do, eating or drinking or anything else, everything should be done to bring glory to God.

The Jesus generation is embarked on a great adventure!

15
GETTING IT ALL TOGETHER

On every hand we hear that "the world is coming apart"; "the global village is about to disintegrate"; "New York is a city without glue"; "the human race is ripping open at the seams." Throughout this book we have dealt with the divisive forces which are corrupting the human race. They augur the disintegration of civilization into bits and pieces, a civilization which man has tried to construct carefully during the last few thousand years. A well-informed congressman told me recently: "Our world is finished. I've given up. I'm just going to try to enjoy what time we have left." For some inexplicable reason, many of the Western world's leaders share this death wish.

Looking ahead, young people want to know: Who can "get it all together"? Who can bring "togetherness" — universal peace and harmony? It is the old story of Humpty Dumpty: "Is there anyone who can pick up the pieces and assemble them into a meaningful and beautiful whole?"

The answer is Jesus Christ. "In Christ all the building fitly framed *together*," wrote Paul to the Ephesians. "As Jesus' followers, we are certain of the future!" In First Thessalonians we have this promise, that "The Lord himself shall descend from heaven with a shout ... and the dead in Christ shall rise first: Then we which are alive and remain shall be caught up *together* with them in the clouds, to meet the Lord in the air: and so shall we ever be with the Lord" (4: 16, 17).

As I look at the United Nations, at America, at Russia, at China, at Great Britain, or even at the human race, I find little reason for hope. But my hope does not rest in the affairs of this world. It rests in Christ who is coming again. The Apostle Paul once said: "If in this life only we have hope . . . we are of all men most miserable." He looked toward another life, and so do I. Concerning the future, there can be absolute certainty and assurance.

When Jesus enters the human scene, we discover that togetherness and hope are things that happen immediately. Upon our receiving Him as Savior and Lord, we are together with Him and have a certain hope concerning the future. When we meet in His name *together* with other like-minded believers, we are bonded *together* with each other, whether we are Americans or Russians, black or white, red or yellow Christians. Jesus Christ has put us all *together*.

At some time in the future, then, these two dimensions of relationship (with Christ and with each other) are going to be fused into one. We are going to be "caught up *together*" to be with Christ forever! In times of strain, distress, persecution, and suffering, this is our comfort. We are to look forward to that time when there will be no more separation or division; no more night; no more sickness; no more sorrow; no more war; no more crime; no more temptation; and no more death.

The return of Jesus Christ "to get it all together" is one of the most popular themes in the minds of today's youth. Whenever I visit a university campus, if there is a question period, this theme is almost certain to arise. In the late sixties the Gallup poll revealed that an overwhelming majority of Americans believed that Jesus Christ is coming back to earth again — and a majority of the clergymen believed it, too.

A few years ago the Bible teaching about the Second Coming of Christ was thought of as "doomsday" preaching. But not any more. It is the only ray of hope that shines as an ever brightening beam in a darkening world. Once leaders felt that technology, science, and ethical education would enable man to work out his own human dilemmas — without God — and establish an ideal society. No serious thinker believes that today.

It is true that many people have some sense of security, but it is a false sense. They believe that man and his works are slowly and painfully making their way upward by their own strength and intelligence. Many who support this theory also claim to believe in the Second Coming of Christ, but they claim that this refers only to the day when man will have purified himself by his own means. They say man will come to recognize the futility of war, the stupidity of greed and selfish behavior, the uselessness of prejudice and intolerance. They say man will understand that he is his brother's keeper and must live according to the Golden Rule.

This so-called theory of inevitable progress is a myth and nothing more. It is based on what man hopes is happening and not on what is really happening. When these "logicians" point to the fact that modern science is now making it possible for us to live longer than our ancestors, they overlook the proposition that death is still our ultimate destiny. At best, we have only been able to postpone it for a few years.

Certain political leaders are dreaming and hoping that the East and the West can be brought together in a future world of brotherhood and that we can take the best of the East and the best of the West and put it all together in a universal utopia. This, too, is a pipe dream. As always, human nature is the flaw. Experience tells us that greed, lust, and selfishness will continue to rear their ugly heads. The Bible teaches that a time of peace will eventually come, but the peace will be imposed by the Antichrist — by the coming of a world dictator. It will last but a short time, and then the world will enter a period in which the judgments of God fall upon the human race. This period will culminate in Armageddon, in a confrontation between the forces of good and the forces of evil which could exterminate the human race. But God, the Bible teaches, will intervene to conclude our age.

From one end to the other, the Bible teaches that our present epoch will end with God's judgment and the return of Jesus Christ to set up His Kingdom. This does not mean the end of the world. It means the end of this age, the end of the domination of evil. Over and over again, the Bible emphasizes the return of Jesus Christ. In Isaiah 66:15 we read that "The Lord will come with fire, and with his chariots like a whirlwind, to render his anger with fury, and his rebuke with flames of fire."

In Jeremiah, we are told that at the Lord's coming Jerusalem will be made the throne of His glory and nations shall be gathered in representation. There will be a mighty disarmament conference in Jerusalem, far greater than any the world has ever seen in Washington or London or Paris!

Ezekiel tells of Jerusalem which is to be restored, a temple which is to be rebuilt, and a land which is to be reclaimed and filled with prosperity.

Daniel saw Jesus in visions, coming as the Judge and King of the earth.

Habakkuk shows the King measuring the new Kingdom with a measuring rod and all the hills bowing to Him.

Zephaniah gives us the new song that He will teach to Israel and describes the overthrow of the false Christ.

Haggai tells of the shaking of all things and only the things of God remaining.

The Old Testament is brimming with many other accounts of His Second Coming.

In the New Testament similar predictions are even more vivid. Matthew likens Christ to a bridegroom coming to receive his bride.

Mark sees Him as a householder going on a long journey and committing certain tasks to his servants until his return.

To Luke, Jesus is a nobleman going to a far country to transact certain businesses and leaving his possessions with his servants that they may trade with them until he comes.

John quotes Christ as saying, "I go and prepare a place for you, I will come again, and receive you unto myself."

In First Corinthians, Paul tells of the Lord's coming to awaken and raise the dead. Second Corinthians describes the new house we shall have when this earthly house is dissolved.

In First Thessalonians, Paul tells us to wait for God's Son from heaven. In Second Thessalonians he gives us the glorious picture of the Lord coming with His saints.

John makes this great promise to all believers. "Now are we the sons of God, and it doth not yet appear what we shall be: but we know that, when he shall appear, we shall be like him, for we shall see him as he is."

The entire Book of Revelation is given over to the teaching of the Second Coming of Jesus Christ.

The most glorious truth in all the world is the Second Coming of Jesus Christ. When minds are full of pessimism and gloom, when all seems lost, it represents the promise of a wonderful future. Many people wail, "What is to become of us? Where are we drifting?" To which the Bible gives a sure, straight answer, saying that the consummation of all things shall be the coming again of Jesus Christ and the rewards that await the elect of God!

Yours is not the first generation of young people to inquire into the future in search of clues of what life will be like tomorrow. Before Jesus Christ was crucified, His disciples asked Him, "What events will signal your return and the end of the world?" Jesus told them, "Don't let anyone fool you" (Matthew 24). And with this, He gave them a summary of events that would signal His return and the end of the world, as we know it. Naming conditions that would prevail one day, He said that we are to watch and prepare. Reading them, one must be struck by their resemblance to what we see daily on our television screens and in our newspapers.

They are the very events that are shattering our society

and civilization, and they will continue to plague us without ceasing until He returns.

What conditions does He mention? He named many "signs." I can mention only a few.

First He said, "For many will come claiming to be the Messiah, and will lead many astray." When I was a teenager, a generation ago, I never heard of anyone having the impertinence to claim to be a messiah. Today such pretenders are commonplace. Khrushchev once described himself as the Christ of Russia. When our Ping-Pong players came back from China, the thing that impressed them most was the fact that Mao Tse-tung was a messiah to 750,000,000 citizens. Here in the West, it was once Timothy Leary, or John Lennon, or Che Guevara. "Messiah counting" is a preoccupation of our times.

It will get worse as "many antichrists" and "messiahs" become forerunners of the ultimate Antichrist. Walter Lippman and Arnold Toynbee are only two of the many who have been telling us that a world anarchy can be controlled only by a super ruler. One of Toynbee's most quoted predictions is, "By making more and more lethal weapons, and at the same time making the world more and more interdependent economically, technology has brought mankind to such a degree of distress that we are ripe for the deifying of any Caesar who might succeed in giving the world unity and peace."

The Bible describes this coming dictator in detail. Read the second chapter of Second Thessalonians and the thirteenth chapter of Revelation. He will rule for a short time. At first, he will bring peace and will be praised by all peoples. He will speak to the entire human race simultaneously. Before television and satellites in space, this could not happen.

Jesus said that *a second sign* would be: "Ye shall hear of wars and rumors of wars; see that you be not troubled: for all these things must come to pass" (Matthew 24:6). It is estimated that thirty times more space is devoted by our major newspapers to wars and rumors of wars today than when I was a teen-ager. But Jesus predicted further that "nation will rise against nation, and kingdom against kingdom." One hundred years ago, we usually had one nation fighting against another nation. World Wars I and II were fought by kingdoms against kingdoms. Today, when pundits write of World War III, they say that no section of the "global village" can escape. The Bible calls this final war by the name of Armageddon. It stands for a time when the whole world will be involved in a showdown that will focus in the Middle East. Before man exterminates himself, however, the Bible promises that the final phase of Christ's Second Coming will be consummated when He returns to establish His Kingdom, that glorious place and time when the lion and the lamb can lie down together.

"Blessed are the peacemakers," Jesus said, but He added that man's own efforts at peacemaking would never succeed until His return as the true Peacemaker. During our time, great demonstrations for peace have attracted 250,000 or more people. These events are not wrong. They display right desires. Peace is being emphasized in our times as never before. But Jesus taught that even the most conscientious efforts are bound to fail until the day He returns. The Apostle Paul wrote: "For when they shall say, Peace and safety; then sudden destruction cometh upon them, as travail upon a woman with child; and they shall not escape" (1 Thessalonians 5:3).

Jesus declared that His return is essential, for it alone can prevent man's selfish quest for power from resulting in the annihilating of the whole human race. Said Jesus: "It will be a time of great distress, such as has never been from the beginning of the world until now, and will never be again. If that time of troubles were not cut short, no living thing could survive; but for the sake of God's chosen it will be cut short."

Christ is truly coming! Most people are aware of the thermonuclear weaponry stockpiled throughout the world today.

Despite highly publicized "bans" on the making and use of armaments, all of us know that enough warheads are around to exterminate the race. They rove in the oceans aboard submarines, they sit in "ready to trigger" missile bases around the world. And now space platforms are being constructed that will carry them overhead. I believe that these are some of the circumstances that Jesus said would bring "distress of nations" and would be the cause of "men's hearts failing them for fear."

Read these words of Peter the fisherman (neither a scholar nor a scientist) and reflect on what scientists are saying: "The day of the Lord will come," predicted Peter, amidst a "great rushing sound, the elements will disintegrate in flames, and the earth with all that is in it will be laid bare." The Russian scientists claim that one of their H-bomb explosions generated heat two and a half times hotter than the center of the sun. Only in our generation has the realization of such a prediction as Peter's been possible.

The *third sign* was that His coming would be preceded by terrible "famines." With the world's population now approaching four billion, and with predictions that it will double during the next generation, though it has slowed down in America, biologists tell us that there is now no way for hungry, "have not" nations (where the population explosion is out of hand) to be fed. Read William and Paul Paddock or Julian Huxley. Read the writings of Stanford biologist Paul Ehrlich or Ohio State's Bruce Griffing. They give the world a decade until famine is universal. They give us a generation-and-a-half to find the means to survive if we are to endure as a race, wholly from the point of view of food.

Note that Jesus spoke of famines developing "in many places," but not universally. We have them now. Ten thousand humans are starving to death each day, the experts say, which is as many deaths in five days as all the American soldiers who perished in Vietnam over the last ten years.

And this is happening despite huge food surpluses in some parts of our world.

Do you believe that Jesus Christ is going to permit this terrible hunger to go on worsening? The Bible says that He will not; He will return to rectify matters.

The *fourth sign* would be "earthquakes in place after place." One newspaper, over a two-year period, recently reported an earthquake happening somewhere in the world on every day except four. To believers in Jesus, each of these is a reminder that Christ is coming soon. In 1970, when Peru experienced the greatest natural disaster in the history of South America, with some 48,000 persons losing their lives, we were reminded again that Jesus Christ is coming back. A professional seismologist has estimated that there has been more than a 2000 percent increase in major earthquakes in the mid-twentieth century over the mid-fifteenth.

The *fifth sign* before His coming would be "multiplied lawlessness and iniquity." I need not enlarge on our current epidemic of crime and violence which has swelled to terrifying proportions. Compared to when I was a boy, we now live in reverse. The people are locked up in their homes at night and the criminals are outside on the loose! When I was young, the criminals were locked up and the people were free to move about. That time has passed for many cities.

In a passage that is startling to many modern eyes, Paul described conditions that would introduce the return of Jesus.

> . . . the *final age* of this world is to be a time of troubles. Men will love nothing but money and self; they will be arrogant, boastful, and abusive; with no respect for parents, no gratitude, no piety, no natural affection; they will be implacable in their hatreds, scandal mongers, intemperate and fierce, strangers to all goodness, traitors, adventurers, swollen with self importance. They will be men who put pleasure in the place of God, men who preserve the outward form of religion, but are a standing denial of its reality. . . .

wicked men and charlatans will make progress from bad to worse, deceiving and deceived (2 Timothy 3:1-5, 13, NEB).

Is this America today? It reads astonishingly like the report of a Presidential Commission describing the factors that corrupt and pervert our society.

As the *sixth sign,* Jesus said: "As it was in the days of Noah, so shall it be also in the days of the Son of man. They did eat, they drank, they married wives, they were given in marriage" (Luke 17:26, 27). Despite God's warnings through Noah, people were so occupied with themselves and with their wickedness that they "knew not until the flood came, and took them all away" (Matthew 24:39). I need not remind you that the world is on an immoral binge such as was not known even in the days of Rome. We are offered every pleasure that man can enjoy and we have abused every gift God ever gave us, including sex, until we no longer find joy and satisfaction in them. We are now trying every perversion to get kicks. This is human nature turned godless, and it is one of the signs of the end.

The seventh sign — one that Bible scholars have looked upon as the most certain sign of all — has taken place within the lifetime of many college students. This sign is the return of the Jews to their ancient homeland! The modern state of Israel was established in May, 1948. In June, 1967, Jerusalem became a Jewish city for the first time since 586 B.C. Jesus had predicted, "Jerusalem shall be trodden down by the Gentiles until the times of the Gentiles be fulfilled." Dr. Wilbur Smith, the great Bible teacher, once told me, "If you ever wake up some morning and find the Israeli armies have occupied Old Jerusalem, you can know that the end is near."

The eighth sign is the rise of Russia as a super power. In the thirty-eighth and thirty-ninth chapters of Ezekiel one can read some of the most fascinating passages in the entire Bible. Many Bible scholars believe that these chapters refer to a "northern" alliance headed by Russia that will appear at the end of the age.

The ninth sign is the emergence of Japan and China and other nations of the Far East. An interesting passage in Revelation 16:12 refers to "the kings of the East." It indicates that a time will come when the Euphrates River will be dried up and the kings of the East will cross toward the West with forces numbering 200,000,000. The Euphrates River is mentioned in the Bible as existing at the time of the Garden of Eden. Such famous cities as ancient Babylon, Nippur, and Ur were later located along its banks. It was the eastern limit of the Roman Empire. It is generally considered to be the boundary between the East and the West. Many Biblical scholars believe that when the "kings of the East" invade the West, the Battle of Armageddon will be near.

All the above signs seem to be converging for the first time in history. Despite rumors of war and prophecies of disaster, we are not to lose heart. For Jesus said that "when these things *begin* to occur, look up and lift up your heads because your deliverance is drawing near."

This is *good* news! His words mean that we should look up *now!* For I believe that Christ will take all of us who have put our trust in Him to heaven before the earth suffers the apocalyptic woes that are described in detail in the Book of Revelation.

After the Great Tribulation during which judgment after judgment will pour down upon a human race whose heart is getting harder and harder toward God, the Bible teaches that the armies of the world will be gathered at Armageddon. Then, as the human race is about to destroy itself in one final conflict, Jesus Christ will return and "get it all together."

For the Christian, all is not hopeless unless his affections are centered on the things of this world. If you have been living a life dedicated to God, laying up treasures in heaven with your affection given to things above, then you have no cause for despair and discouragement. Christians may now be approaching our finest hour! After hearing a clergyman preach on the Second Coming of Christ, Queen Victoria once said, "I wish He would come during my lifetime so that I could take my crown and lay it at His feet."

What a moment to take the newspaper in one hand and the Bible in the other and watch the unfolding of the great drama of the ages. This is an exciting and thrilling time to be alive. I would not want to live in any other period.

Jesus said: "Therefore be ye also ready: for in such an hour as ye think not the Son of man cometh" (Matthew 24: 44).

Are you ready to meet Him if He should come today? In many places the Bible advises us to be ready always. One can say that this is an appeal based on fear. "By faith Noah being warned of God of things not seen as yet, moved with fear, prepared an ark to the saving of his house" (Hebrews 11:7). The word "fear" could be translated terrified. Noah was so terrified at the prospect of coming events that his fear drove him to build the ark. Surely, we should be similarly moved.

Not only are we to be ready; we are to intensify our work for Christ. Jesus said: "Blessed is that servant, whom his lord when he cometh shall find so doing" (Matthew 24:46).

Some people believe that if Christ is really coming, why carry on? Why not quit work and watch? This was one of the problems to which Paul addressed himself when he wrote to the Thessalonians. Explaining some of the details of the last days, he urged them *to get to work*. The hope of the coming of Christ should make us work all the harder so that we shall "not be ashamed before Him at His coming" (I John 2:28). To the Christian, the return of Christ will be a glorious moment. To those outside of Christ it will be the greatest of calamities, a tragic separation, an unbelievable disappointment. It will be hell. But to those who are ready, what a glorious consummation.

In describing the future of Christians, the Apostle Paul once said: "Eye hath not seen, nor ear heard, neither have entered into the heart of man, the things which God hath prepared for them that love him" (1 Corinthians 2:9). What are these wonders? We do not know. Our human capacity for understanding is too limited.

At the close of the Bible, a reader encounters these words: "And I saw a new heaven and a new earth: for the first heaven and the first earth were passed away . . ." (Revelation 21:1).

A new world is coming! Each time we pray the Lord's Prayer, we pray, "Thy Kingdom come, thy will be done on earth as it is in heaven." That prayer will be answered. Heaven is described as a new creation in which we shall move in new bodies, possessed of new names, singing new songs, living in a new city, governed by a new form of government, and challenged by new prospects of eternity with social justice for all. The paradise that man lost will be regained, but it will be much more. It will be a new paradise; not the old one repaired, patched up, and made over. When God says, "Behold, I make all things new," the emphasis is on *all things*. One day we shall live in a brand-new world.

As I write the final words of this book, I recall hearing a song recently sung by Bobby Goldsboro. It epitomizes the new and wonderful thing that is happening to young people all over the world. Its words present the best evidence I have discovered that many of today's youth are truly preparing themselves for tomorrow: "It's time again for Him to come back. . . ."

Yes, Jesus is coming again!

Yes, you can prepare to meet Him.

Yes, you can know positively that He will accept you.

Centuries ago, the apostles greeted each other with the word "Maranatha" — "The Lord is coming."

How about you? How about you being ready to help Him "get it all together?"

Maranatha!

FOOTNOTES

CHAPTER 1

[1] Charles Reich, *The Greening of America* (New York: Random House, 1970).

[2] Leighton Ford, *The Christian Persuader* (London: Hodder and Stoughton, 1967).

[3] Reich, *Greening*.

CHAPTER 2

[1] F. Bronkowski, *Adolescence* (a quarterly), (Roslyn Heights, New York: Libra Publishers).

[2] Seymour M. Lipset and Sheldon S. Wolin, eds., *Berkeley Student Revolt: Facts and Interpretations* (New York: Anchor Books, 1965).

[3] Reich, *Greening*.

CHAPTER 3

[1] J. Robert Moskin, *Morality in America* (New York: Random House, 1966).

CHAPTER 5

[1] Evelyn Duvall, *Why Wait Till Marriage* (London: Hodder and Stoughton, 1966).

[2] Lydia G. Dawes, "The Adolescent, His Conflicts, and Possible Methods of Adjustment," *Psychiatry and Religion*, ed. Joshua Liebman, 1948.

[3] Mary S. Calderone, *Release from Sexual Tension* (London: R. Hale, 1963).

[4] Helen J. Burn, *Better Than the Birds, Smarter Than the Bees* (Nashville, Tenn.: Abingdon Press, 1969).

[5] Ibid.

[6] Norman Vincent Peale, *Sin, Sex, and Self-Control* (Tadworth: World's Work, 1966).

[7] Ibid.

[8] Ibid.

[9] Marion Hilliard, *A Woman Doctor Looks at Love and Life* (London: Macmillan 1958.)

CHAPTER 6

[1] William Hedgepeth, *The Alternative: Communal Life in America* (New York: Macmillan, 1970).

[2] Norman F. Cantor, *The Age of Protest* (New York: Hawthorn Books, 1969).

[3] Ibid.

[4] Alexander Klein, *Natural Enemies: Youth and the Clash of Generations* (Philadelphia: Lippincott, 1970).

[5] Frank R. Donovan, *Wild Kids: How Youth Has Shocked Its Elders Then and Now* (Harrisburg, Penna.; Stackpole Books, 1967).

[6] Theodore Roszak, *The Making of a Counter-Culture* (London: Faber & Faber, 1970.)

CHAPTER 7

[1] *The Journal of Social Issues* (Ann Arbor, Mich.: Society for Psychological Study of Social Issues).

[2] Edgar Z. Friedenberg, *Coming of Age in America* (New York: Random House, 1965).

[3] Jerry Simmons and Barry Winograd, *It's Happening: Portrait of the Youth Scene Today* (Santa Barbara, Calif.: McNally, 1966).

CHAPTER 8

[1] Donovan, *Wild Kids*.

[2] Roszak, *Making Counter-Culture*.

CHAPTER 9

[1] Klein, *Natural Enemies*.

[2] Jose Ortega y Gasset, *Man and Crisis*, tr. by Mildred Adams (New York: Norton, 1958).

[3] Friedenberg, *Coming of Age*.

[4] Paul Wienpahl, *Zen Diary* (New York: Harper and Row, 1970).

CHAPTER 11

[1] Roszak, *Making Counter-Culture*.